The Story of
WMU

Rosalie H. Hunt

Birmingham, Alabama

Woman's Missionary Union, SBC
P. O. Box 830010
Birmingham, AL 35283-0010

For more information, visit our Web site at www.wmu.com or call
1-800-968-7301.

Dewey Decimal Classification: 266.06

Subject Headings: WOMAN'S MISSIONARY UNION, SBC—HISTORY
                  BAPTISTS—HISTORY
                  SOUTHERN BAPTIST CONVENTION—HISTORY

ISBN-10: 1-56309-860-1
ISBN-13: 978-1-56309-860-4
W053105•0905•2.5M1

Design by Janell E. Young and Sherry Hunt
Cover by Cheryl Totty

Unless otherwise noted, all factual information is from Catherine B. Allen,
A Century to Celebrate (Birmingham, AL: Woman's Missionary Union,
1987).

Dedication

To Alice Wells Hall, my mother, who became a Sunbeam in South Carolina in 1907, graduated from WMU Training School in 1927, went to China as a missionary in 1929, and passed on to her daughter a lifelong passion for missions. And, to Alma Hunt, whose spirit and friendship have inspired my enduring devotion to WMU.

Rosalie Hall Hunt

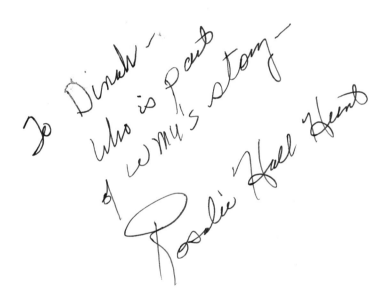

Contents

Preface

The footprints of thousands of women are found in the cement of early Baptist history in America. These are the women who captured a vision of the personal challenge of the Great Commission. Many of their names have been lost in time, but the echo of their passion for missions has reverberated through the centuries, even into the new millennium. Their legacy is alive in this century's Woman's Missionary Union® (WMU®), one of the world's largest missions organizations.

With its inception in 1888, WMU has emphasized passing on a passion for missions to the next generation through both word and example, reminding each new era of a heritage that includes heroic sacrifice and God's timely intercession. The story of WMU and its leaders is an extraordinary venture of faith.

It is important for history's sake to chronicle an organization's significant decisions and achievements. In 1988, Catherine Allen recorded WMU's first 100 years in her book *A Century to Celebrate*. She told about the birth and building of the organization by courageous women throughout the South who had a heart for missions and a vision of the future. In the subsequent two decades since the publication of Allen's book, a host of this-generation women, standing on a firm foundation of passionate heritage and heroic sacrifice, have led WMU to become a publishing company, a consulting firm, and a church services organization for the Baptist denomination, home to Baptist Nursing Fellowship℠ (BNF®), a creative international ministries network, and more.

The Story of WMU connects the past with the present day. WMU's history is made up of thousands of individual stories of women who loved and wept, who experienced joy and victory, but who struggled with setbacks and heartaches in much the same way women experience victory or defeat, pain or joy in this century. No brief history can record each woman's story, but it can tell a few within each generation. The stories told here represent all the women who heard God's Great Commission call and responded within the confines of their times and culture. How they did so is a fascinating account of adaptability and determination. Their stories are an inspiration for those who seek to reach the lost in any generation.

We have included short vignettes of women pivotal to the development of WMU. These women took bold stands to serve as leaders. Their names are synonymous with WMU. Their story is WMU's story. Their impact on the world cannot be overemphasized. However, these women did not stand alone. Thousands of women joined those portrayed in this book in paving the way for our generation to continue carrying out the mandate of the Great Commission in the place where God has put us. Today there are men and women who are sharing the love of Jesus because their great-great-grandmother, aunt, Sunbeam teacher, or GA® leader loved missions.

We invite you to delve into the story of WMU, to explore the journey of courageous women who held one central vision—challenging Christian believers to understand and be personally involved in the mission of God. As you read *The Story of WMU*, we hope that you will be inspired to join the venture of faith and discover the plan that God has designed especially for you to be personally involved in missions—for you too have a legacy to pass on.

Through the years, WMU has become many things, and still the voice of Annie Armstrong, the first corresponding secretary of Woman's Missionary Union, rings out: "The future lies all before us . . . a leap forward, to altitudes of endeavor and success undreamed of before."

1
1792–1877

WMU's story began in the hearts of women long before the birth of the organization in 1888. It actually began far from American shores, in the quiet little town of Kettering, England. The beginning indeed involved a woman, for the woman affectionately known as Widow Wallis provided the little back parlor of her lovely Georgian-style home for a historic meeting. Widow Wallis was gracious hostess to the 14 young men who met on a blustery gray October afternoon in 1812 and formed the Baptist Missionary Society of Great Britain.[1] That meeting marked the beginning of the modern missions movement. William Carey, who was there that day, volunteered to go to India. Carey went on to blaze a new trail and came to be called the father of modern missions.[2]

Carey's vision was just the beginning. After a century of exploration in the Americas, the world seemed to be steadily shrinking, and a contagious new excitement about missions flourished. It spread to the fledgling United States of America. Its citizens already understood the ideals of organizing for common causes, and this eventually became a spur for missions efforts. Both men and women formed missions associations, and a number of these supported William Carey and work in India.

Woman's Missionary Union descended from a group that was formed in New York in November 1797 and led by Isabella Graham, a devout Presbyterian. The next recorded woman's organization is the one that actually launched the first and largest woman's movement in history.

The heroine of the story is the most unlikely, a tiny 21-year-old paralyzed woman. This frail young visionary, Mary "Polly" Webb, was inspired by the Bible admonition to "be ye strong therefore, and let not your hands be weak." Polly was a new Baptist member of Boston's Second Baptist Church and in 1800 organized the Boston Female Society for Missionary Purposes with seven other Baptists and six Congregationalists. Their purpose was to pray and collect money for missions. William Carey was one of those who received their support. The Baptist members were the biggest givers and eventually took over the organization.

The earliest record of a woman's missionary society in the South was the Wadmalaw and Edisto Female Mite Society in South Carolina. They were reporting contributions by 1811. A year later, about 20 such societies had been organized. That year, Polly Webb sent out a plan for other women to organize and join them in prayer for missions. Women in many of the 18 states existing in 1812 answered the rallying cry and soon more than 100 such groups were praying for missions.

The spread of such groups was galvanized by news that the first missionaries from America had sailed. They sailed in two groups on separate ships, both headed to India. Ann and Adoniram Judson were in the first group; Luther Rice followed soon after. The three young missionaries left America as Congregationalists but by conviction became Baptists while en route to the missions field.

The Judsons pioneered the spread of the gospel in Burma and became mythic figures in nineteenth-century Christianity.[3] Luther Rice returned to America to rally Baptists and stir up support. This young bachelor traveled from Maine to South Carolina, urging Baptist congregations to organize and support the newly baptized Judsons as their first missionaries. This led to the historic Triennial Baptist Convention which met in May 1814 in Philadelphia. That month Baptists in America became a denomination. The rallying cry? *Missions.*[4]

Missionary Societies and Baptist Organization

Female missionary societies blossomed, even before many of the states had a Baptist convention. In fact, women's missionary societies sent men to help organize state conventions, as the culture of the times did not allow women delegates. Over half the groups who sent delegates in 1823 to organize the Alabama Baptist State Convention were women's groups.

When the Triennial Convention was born in 1814, there were 17 known women's societies that were active. But by the time the convention met again in 1817, 110 of the 187 missionary societies which had formed were women's groups.

In 1845, Baptists in the South formed their own convention. There were more than 100 female societies by this time, but such groups were only in slightly more than 2 percent of the total number of churches. The Foreign Mission Board (now International Mission Board) and the Board of Domestic Missions (later Home Mission Board and now North American Mission Board) were created at the 1845 organizational meeting of Southern Baptists. The formation of the Southern Baptist Convention (SBC) seems to have foreshadowed the Civil War.

Baptist historian Bill Leonard states: "The organization of the Southern Baptist Convention demonstrates the impact of American denominational influences on a highly regionalized religious community. The links between Southern culture and Southern Baptist denomination consciousness were deep, if not inseparable."[5]

This new southern split did not encourage women to organize. One reason for this reluctance was what was happening in the North just then. Northern women were organizing and speaking out against slavery. The proslavery leadership in the South doubtless thought this "bad example" could lead to too much power for women, so they condemned antislavery groups and along with that discouraged any women's groups.

Nor did southern women have dynamic missionary women to rally around. Ann Judson was no more. Dozens of early mission societies had been named for Ann Hasseltine Judson (as well as Judson College in Alabama), but the heroic Ann had died far away, as had Henrietta Hall Shuck of Virginia, America's first woman in China.

Although the trend towards forming southern women's groups slowed down, it did not stop. About the time the Civil War began, Sarah Doremus (who belonged to the Dutch Reform Church in New York), began the Woman's Union Missionary Society, which involved women of several denominations, including Baptists. Their goal was "to send out single women untrammeled by family cares to Christianize heathen women who cannot be reached by men missionaries."

Even the use of *Woman* in the name was a pioneering move. Up until this time, women's organizations were *Female*. Woman's Union Missionary Society began by supporting Sarah Hall Marston, a single Baptist missionary to Burma.[6] WUMS was unable to impact the South, however, until the furor of war ended. By then, Congregationalists and Northern Methodist women's societies had organized, along with Northern Presbyterians, to appoint and support women missionaries.

The War's Effects

The Civil War brought death and deprivation that threatened every aspect of life, including church efforts.

Contributions to the mission-sending agencies sank to a fraction of prewar levels. The FMB had to plan carefully to get moneys across "enemy" lines to fund missionaries and their work. When funding didn't come, foreign missionaries took secular jobs, and home missionaries joined the Confederate army as chaplains.

Even churches became battlefields. The American Baptist Home Mission Society (northern), with permission of the United States government, seized several Southern Baptist church buildings during the war. The SBC was slow to forgive this kind of affront. Other church property was damaged, neglected, or outright destroyed. Times were perilous and tragic.

Such gloom could have altogether ended the growth of women's societies and missions expansion. Instead, economic destitution gave women new leadership roles. Dire poverty afforded women a chance to prove their abilities. Necessity made them nurses, farmers, teachers, tradespersons, and church leaders. The same necessity made most males accept women's initiatives. As a result, women worked towards education, marketable skills, and equitable pay. They often were the ones who assumed financial support of their churches.

> For years after the Civil War, foreign missions contributions fell short of prewar levels. Families who had previously contributed generously were now destitute and using all their earnings to build back their lives. The number of home missionaries plunged to an all-time low in 1876. Missions took a temporary backseat to survival and priorities were not reversed until after the South's federal military occupation ended in 1877.

History appears to confirm that times of drastic social upheaval are the best times for women to take on new roles. This was certainly true for intrepid Baptist women in the Reconstruction South. Women formed ladies aid societies to meet the many needs around them. Called by various names, societies had existed prior to the war, but their number increased in order to rescue congregations. Through sewing circles and other means, women earned or solicited money, repairing dilapidated church buildings, paying off mortgages, and buying stoves and lights. The women paid pastors, including many who had not been paid fully in years. Women bought music instruments, dispensed food to the hungriest, tended the sick, sheltered orphans, and befriended those who had lost their place in society. They even lightened the gloom through fund-raising entertainment.

However, these early societies generally did not back fund-raising events as the way to get income, and they did not pass such a precedent to their "offspring," the Woman's Missionary Union of the future.

Nor did all the magnificent work of the aid societies translate into a voice for women to influence church decisions. Although Baptist churches were supposedly democratic, women usually had no church business vote. They could not speak before the congregation other than to give a statement of faith for church membership. And, they were prohibited from speaking before church councils.

Defeat in the Civil War, Reconstruction humiliation, and cultural devastation led many male southerners to become even more entrenched in their philosophy of women, that all women should be quiet, gentle, and restrained. Southern men glorified the Lost Cause. In a region reeling from defeat, they resembled survivors clinging to traditions that were like shattered pieces of a sinking ship.

Although it is difficult to imagine in this new millennium, churches in the South in the late 1860s did not have weekly preaching, suppers, weekly offerings, choirs, or youth activities. Hardly any even had Sunday Schools, so many men regarded a separate "women's" organization as a threat to the "southern way of life," feeling they might threaten local independence. Anything new was suspect and many church leaders looked upon women's groups as competition. Some men believed women already controlled the wealth, and, if organized, they would divert money from the local church. Some men even had a fear of women "leaving home and entering the pulpit." After all, look at northern trends. The women's rights movement, suffrage, women lectures, and Woman's Mission to Woman all seemed threatening to a way of life that was the only thing left for some to cling to.

The passion against women's organizations also grew from biblical interpretation of women's roles and from the desire to glue shattered southern culture back together. As southerners gained distance from the war, many hid humiliation under traditional pride. The glorification of the Lost Cause, the mythological Old South, and the code of chivalry drew Southern Baptists into roles that didn't accommodate women leaders.

Numbers of Southern Baptist men, in sweeping generalizations, stated that "our women" did not want to be public speakers and did not want organization or rights. Therefore, they reasoned, only outside agitators and misguided men could be pushing such ideas.

The Tiny Box Solution

Lingering mourning and poverty in the South retarded the development of any women's movements, but mission societies were the first structured groups built by postwar southern women. Necessity propelled change and women's resourcefulness in raising church money caught the eye of the Foreign Mission Board, which of course was left destitute by the war. Secretary James B. Taylor issued a survival call to the "Baptist ladies of the South." His circular letter asked for a ladies' committee from each church to gather offerings.

The primary means of collecting these offerings was the mite box. Women were challenged to place two cents in a specific little box on the first day of each week. Up until then most offerings were just made annually. The idea of "mites" seemed infinitely more doable, even though money was a rare commodity in the post–Civil War South. Little garnet-colored boxes with gold lettering spread throughout the South. As a direct result, regular funds began to flow to the FMB. In 10 years the FMB had furnished 28,520 mite boxes at a cost of $733.40. Those little boxes reaped $75,000 in return.

The guiding light behind these little boxes was the remarkable Ann Jane Graves of Baltimore. She died in 1878, exactly 10 years before WMU was officially born, but her amazing spirit and passion for missions was one reason this historic union ever drew its first breath. This brilliant Methodist intellectual became a Baptist in 1868, and her impact on an entire denomination lives on.[7]

> In a day when a woman would walk a mile rather than spend two cents on a postage stamp, mite boxes were filled by sacrifice. Women came up with all sorts of ways to raise money for their mite boxes. Some did sewing. Others raised money by selling butter, vegetables, and poultry. Eggs laid on Sunday could be sold for missions. The ability of women to preserve the mission boards through the mite box seemed to further irritate a vocal segment of Southern Baptist leadership. Their evident talent in managing money challenged "proper roles." Many men thought that single women knew nothing about money, so the treasurer for each group was usually a married woman. Furthermore, so few women had banking opportunities that husbands or pastors had to assist them in sending the mission boards their hard-earned mite box money.

Graves's son Rosewell was one of the first Baptist missionaries to China and his firsthand news from the field fired his mother to gather women to pray and to give. Through her efforts, Woman's Mission to Woman was born in Baltimore in 1871—the first widely influential organization among Southern Baptist women.[8] She was indeed the first to gather together the initial women's meeting at a Southern Baptist Convention. The Convention met in Baltimore that year of 1868. In some years, women had been allowed to observe the meetings from a balcony. This year, Ann brought together women who had accompanied their husbands to Baltimore and she quietly met with them in the balcony. Her message to them was to go home and organize. And, the founding of WMU in 1888 grew directly from the seed Ann Graves planted as she roused and united Southern Baptist women.[9]

Southern Women Organize

Mite boxes and ladies aid organizations led to bigger things. Something that became an enduring pattern among Baptist women was a missionary speaker to inform and inspire. In 1869, Ann Baker Graves invited a furloughing Methodist missionary to India, Harriet Brittan, to speak in Baltimore. The missionary addressed a large audience that included many Baptists. They were so challenged by her thrilling story that Baltimore Baptist women decided to found their own Woman's Union Missionary Society.

Consequently, in 1870, the Baltimore branch of Woman's Union Missionary Society was born, but reorganized just a year later as an all-Baptist society, renaming themselves Woman's Mission to Woman. Their goal was "to give light to the women that sit in darkness because of Bible destitution, by taking the gospel of Christ in their homes, through the agency of native Bible-women, aided and superintended by their Christian sisters from Bible lands."

This new group, with Graves at the helm as corresponding secretary, asked if they could work with the

Ann Baker Graves

 She died before it was born, but Ann Graves carved her name forever into the foundation of Woman's Missionary Union. Born into a Methodist family in 1804, she did not become a Baptist until 1868, the same year she gathered together the Baptist women in Baltimore, her home city.

Young Ann Baker was a brilliant and articulate student, an introspective and reflective intellectual. She received her diploma in 1821, the top student in her class. Ann accepted the proposal of physician John Graves of New York when she was 27, on the condition he would move to Baltimore. He did.

Ann had seven children during the following 16 years and yet found time to write. She was the author of several influential books.

In time, one of her own children became a big influence on her. Rosewell H. Graves was the first physician sent to China by the Southern Baptist Foreign Mission Board. He and his mother carried on a prolific correspondence and she in turn enlisted women to pray for missions. Out of her skilled leadership, Baltimore's Woman's Mission to Woman was born, the first widely influential organization of Southern Baptist women.

Ann borrowed on her Methodist background for promotional ideas, including the amazingly successful mite box. And in large part due to her influence, the Foreign Mission Board reversed policy and appointed single women missionaries.

Ann Baker Graves planted the seeds from which WMU grew. One of her recruits, Martha McIntosh, became WMU's first national president, and later said of Ann Baker Graves, "It would be impossible in writing a history of woman's mission work in the South to omit Mrs. Ann J. Graves, the originator and moving spirit of the work."

From *Laborers Together with God* by Catherine Allen (WMU, 1987).

FMB, supplying input along with money. James Taylor, the longtime secretary of the Board, didn't show any acceptance of input, just of money. But shortly after Woman's Mission to Woman was founded, Taylor died, and was succeeded by Henry Allen Tupper, who promptly reversed the Board's policy. This talented and sensitive Charlestonian made room in foreign missions for women. Through the years to come, he and Lottie Moon became lifelong friends who shared a deep commitment to the cause of the Great Commission.

That same year, 1872, the FMB gave approval for 21-year-old Edmonia Moon of Virginia, to go as a self-supporting missionary to China, living with regularly appointed missionaries in Tengchow. Tupper suggested that the Baptist women of Richmond organize on Edmonia's behalf, which they did in April 1872.[10] This was a period of fast development in the growth of mission spirit. The largest group of foreign missionaries in Southern Baptist history assembled in Baltimore that same month to sail for China. Edmonia Moon sailed with them.

Of course, along with the excitement of so many new missionaries was the need to adequately support them. This need merely added impetus to the spirit igniting Southern Baptist women.

Societies Expand

The concept of WMU seemed to erupt nearly simultaneously in various parts of Southern Baptist territory. Women's societies grew through both family and friend connections. The very month that Baltimore women organized, a similar society was born at First Baptist Church, Newberry, South Carolina. Mothers and sisters, friends, and even pastors shared information and mite boxes. Groups began in Louisiana, Florida, Alabama, North Carolina, and Missouri.

Actually, by 1872, these women had as effective a foreign missions effort as any denomination in the North. And this effort was uniquely southern in flavor. Every corner of the Convention had a permanent women's organization, with Baltimore mothering them all.

Lottie Moon

Charlotte "Lottie" Digges Moon was a most unlikely missionary. Born into privilege in 1840, she was schooled in academics and social graces. She gained a reputation as both an intellectual and as a lighthearted skeptic. It was during college, however, that Lottie professed faith in Christ and the purpose of her life was completely altered. Although sensing the call of God, she was single, and single women were not appointed as missionaries. She became a teacher and began a girls' school, supplementing her family's income which had been devastated by the Civil War.

Then in 1872, in response to pleas from Woman's Mission to Woman in Baltimore, the Foreign Mission Board permitted Lula Whilden to accompany her married sister to China, and sanctioned Edmonia Moon, Lottie's sister, to go to China as a self-supporting missionary, assisting a missionary family there. And shortly thereafter, in 1873, Lottie Moon became the first single woman officially appointed by the FMB, and what a standard she set.

Lottie first studied the language, applying her superb linguistic skills to the arduous task and quickly becoming fluent in the language. Next, she organized girls' schools, but she could not forget the masses in the countryside who had never heard the good news. She broadened her field, spending the majority of her time in the villages around Tengchow. Her work was most effective and her biggest regret was the vastness of the need and the dearth of missionaries.

Her work was felt thousands of miles away. Lottie's letters home inspired countless women's missionary societies. They were amazed that such a cultured woman would live in a dangerous, heathen land. Lottie's fascinating letters ranged from descriptive travelogues to desperate pleas for financial support and more workers to come.

Mobs, murders, disease, dirt, street sewage, and sickness drove many missionaries, including her sister Edmonia, to emotional and physical breakdown. In 1876, Lottie took her sister home, then rushed back to China.

Living Chinese-style in the interior, Lottie invented cutting-edge mission strategies. She helped establish a church that became the nucleus of rapid Christian growth. She arbitrated colleagues' disagreements. She trained newcomers.

Lottie Moon met the Chinese people's physical as well as

spiritual needs. When revolution, plague, and famine hit in the first decade of the twentieth century, she bore the burden. Busy younger missionaries did not notice her progressive weakness as she gave away her food.

Meanwhile, the FMB fell into debt, sending notice that funds might be curtailed. Lottie drew on her inheritance and savings to give to her Chinese friends. By the time colleagues realized she had ceased eating, her four-feet-five frame had dropped to 50 pounds. Horrified co-workers sent her back home with a missionary nurse. On Christmas Eve 1912, as her ship lay at anchor in Kobe, Japan, Lottie Moon died.

News of her death washed like a sea of guilt over WMU. Her name became synonymous with the Christmas offering she spawned. Today, the Lottie Moon Christmas Offerings are the largest single source of funding for Southern Baptist International missions.

After her death, the Tengchow Christians erected a stone monument to her memory in the churchyard. That monument concludes with the simple phrase: The *Tengchow Church Remembers Forever.* For 100 years it has survived famine and wars. During the terrible Cultural Revolution of the 1960s and early 1970s, Tengchow believers buried the monument to protect it from the Red Guards. When that period ended and it was safe to do so, the memorial was resurrected and placed once more in the churchyard. It stands there today—mute testimony to a life of service, love, and sacrifice.

Portions from *The New Lottie Moon Story* by Catherine Allen (Broadman Press, 1980).

In 1874, Tupper and the FMB stirred the women to further organization by appointing central committees for women's work in each state. Such a move further strengthened the impact women's missionary groups exerted on missions development.

There was as yet, however, no national coordination of women's interest in Southern Baptist missions work, no formal communications network to learn about missionary needs or missions opportunities; nor was there a channel for sharing ideas or burdens, since there was no national organization. Nevertheless, throughout the

South tiny pinpoints of light began piercing the darkness of missions ignorance and illuminating, step by single step, the path ahead for pioneering women with passion and vision. Peril and pain lay immediately ahead in an unclear future. So did great adventure.

2
1878–1888

Tenacity, patience, and a passion for sharing the good news defined the courageous Baptist women who led fledgling mission societies across the South, both locally and through the central committees in each state. Their Christian sisters pioneering in China missions were a vital spur.

The mother and sisters of J. B. Hartwell, who served in North China, were founders and leaders of mission societies in both South Carolina and Louisiana. One of them inspired Martha McIntosh to leadership in South Carolina, which then led to her becoming the first president of Woman's Missionary Union. Over a 16-year period, Baptist women steadily planted mission societies and, in faith, bided their time—some patiently, some chafing at the snail-like pace but nonetheless working while they waited for God's timing.

Women Save the Mission Boards

By the late 1870s, the leaders of Baptist agencies began to realize that they needed women if they were to secure funding. In 1873, the first fiscal signs of life for the FMB were obvious. Contributions increased by 75 percent; and in later years leaders acknowledged this to be a direct result of Baptist women's initiative. The funds flowing to the Foreign Mission Board (FMB) continued to increase, and the Home Mission Board (HMB), which had only reluctantly acknowledged the women in 1877, was lamenting its lowest giving since the Civil War.

To make matters worse, the FMB considered the HMB as competition, fighting for the same funds. Their methods for raising money were also suspect. They had paid agents who ended up skimming off 44 percent to 53 percent of contributions. Undoubtedly, this unpopular practice reflected poorly on the HMB. Some states even prohibited HMB agents from soliciting funds in their borders.

A turnaround came in 1882 with the providential selection of Isaac Taylor Tichenor to head the HMB. This brilliant, dedicated leader left the presidency of Auburn University, and upon becoming secretary, moved HMB headquarters, from Marion, Alabama to Atlanta, Georgia. Tichenor then asked Annie Armstrong of Baltimore to organize the women to provide clothing for Native Americans at an HMB school in Oklahoma, a school that had been built by her uncle.

A talented visionary, Armstrong became personally involved and committed. In short order Annie Armstrong involved Maryland women in the clothing project, organized the Woman's Baptist Home Missionary Society of Maryland, and became its first president.

Tichenor won credit for saving the Home Mission Board and went down in history as a friend to the women. His wife and daughters were heavily involved in women's societies, so he was very well aware of both their impact and importance.

At the time Tichenor became head of the HMB, only 31 women's societies were sending funds to the Board, but 500 sent money to the FMB. Clearly, there was a sense of competition; but by 1888, Baptist women had moved to a dual commitment. One of the driving forces was the leadership of Annie Armstrong.

Annie Armstrong: 1888–1906

Annie Armstrong, the first corresponding secretary of Woman's Missionary Union, and Lottie Moon, the first fully appointed single woman sent by the FMB, on one rare occasion spoke at the same WMU Annual Meeting. What an amazing contrast it must have been, Annie Armstrong, six feet tall—regal and ramrod straight, standing next to Lottie Moon, a decade older and four feet five inches tall. These two most famous names of early WMU history were both giant pioneer figures who charted the course of Baptist missions history.

Annie Walker Armstrong was born in 1850 in Baltimore, Maryland, into a family noted for influence, character, and strong women. Her mother was one of the founding members of Baltimore's Woman's Mission to Woman organization, but Annie did not personally profess faith until she was 20. That mother's love for missions found deep root in the daughter. When Annie personally planned a drive to provide over 200 summer suits for the students at the HMB's Creek Nation Indian School in Oklahoma, her heart and zeal for missions took wing. Through her efforts and leadership, the clothing was provided and this led to Annie's organizing a group called Woman's Home Mission Society of Maryland, the beginning of Maryland women's direct support of home missions. Annie Armstrong became the first president of Maryland's statewide women's committee.

Annie became secretary and editor-in-chief of the Maryland Baptist Mission Rooms in 1886. Working without pay, she developed a publishing business that became the most extensive missions information bureau of any denomination.

Annie was a powerful advocate of home missions and Martha McIntosh of South Carolina was the same for foreign missions endeavors. Those two women came to the 1888 meeting of women during the SBC in Richmond, determined to organize the missions. Armstrong challenged the women with the question: "What are your marching orders?"

She was selected as the fledgling organization's first corresponding secretary and history has proven her God's woman for that time and place. WMU's far-reaching vision and ministries are in great part the legacy of Annie Walker Armstrong. Almost single-handedly she created a missions consciousness among Southern Baptists. Her innovative ideas of promoting missions sparked a veritable torrent of results that grew through the subsequent years.

Annie created a real connection between missionaries and the Baptist in the pew and also connected the Home and Foreign Mission Boards with the Sunday School Board in the interest of missions.

One of her favorite co-workers nicknamed her Miss Strong Arm, and indeed she was. She was also strong-willed, and time has shown that to be a trait much needed in those precarious early years. Resourceful, persevering, kindhearted, tenacious: all these adjective applied to Annie Armstrong. National WMU president Ethlene Boone Cox, upon the 50th anniversary of WMU, said of Annie Armstrong: "She stamped her life upon her generation and upon generations to come."

As WMU corresponding secretary for 18 years, she laid a bedrock foundation for WMU—involving Southern Baptist women in systematic giving, missions education, consistent missions prayer, a missions publishing business, expansion of Southern Baptist territory, and the organizing of black Baptist women.

This woman who become a Baptist legend, did not disdain "insignificant" work, nor did she ever seem to rest. Working late into the night and on holidays, all without pay, Annie was an indefatigable letter writer. (See Keith Harper's *Rescue the Perishing.*)

Annie loved teaching little ones, and taught children in Sunday School for over 50 years. She intensely disliked travel, but that did not prevent her from making countless trips, covering thousands of miles promoting women's missions work. The single mission point closest to her heart was the work with Native Americans in Oklahoma, and she cherished memories of a trip she was able to make to Oklahoma to witness to the Osage Indians.

No one pretended that pioneering with a woman's organization would be easy. Conflicts arose, but WMU weathered the storms and emerged stronger. Various issues and differences of opinion eventually led to Annie's resignation in 1906. She continued to be active in her local WMU, however, and it was she who in 1918 suggested that the missions offering at Christmas be named for Lottie Moon. When in 1934 Southern Baptist women voted to name the home missions offering for Annie Armstrong who had pioneered home missions emphases among women, she agreed with great reluctance.

WMU continued to grow in strength following Annie's resignation, in large part because of her visionary work in building it with such deep and lasting roots. Annie Armstrong's life was a legacy. This amazing woman was truly a visionary dreamer, one who was a mighty advocate and mover of missions. The list of her accomplishments is extraordinary—from the seeds she sowed for a fully age-graded missions organization in churches, to the firm base of financial support for missions through the missions boards, to the promotion of personal and local involvement of women in missions.

Annie Armstrong died December 20, 1938, but not before sending a beautiful letter of benediction and challenge to WMU on its 50th anniversary. Annie stated her heart's desire for them: "After the study of God's word comes study of the fields, then people pray—then they give. . . . Speak unto the children of Israel that they go forward."

Portions from *Annie Armstrong: Dreamer in Action* by Bobbie Sorrill (Broadman Press, 1984) and *Laborers Together with God* by Catherine Allen (WMU, 1987).

Women Organize to Meet Needs

The struggling economy of the South showed signs of revival by 1880, and Baptist women looked at new ways they could relieve suffering beyond their own families and the local church. Gateway cities had great needs as immigrants flooded into the ports and farm families left their overworked lands to search for jobs in factories and mills. Masses of poor men, women, and children crowded into the cities and usually met dire conditions. Women missionaries went to their aid, sustained by Southern Baptist women who had become eager volunteers.

New missions work, however, required coordination, and Baptist women realized anew their need for a central organization to guide them. They were frustrated to do so much work and yet not be allowed to attend the annual Convention meeting as delegates or serve on committees. Nonetheless, a growing fraternity of sympathetic pastors in each state encouraged these visionary women and did their Convention talking for them.

Then, in what appeared to be an impediment, the Southern Baptist Convention in 1881 recommended the

Foreign Mission Board employ a woman to superintend and promote women's work, but the Board declined. This rejection made women leaders determined to continue to press for recognition as an organization.

Over the next 6 years, step-by-step, a foundation was laid that would lead to a national, united women's missions organization. Along with supportive pastors, publications gave voice to Baptist women's efforts to organize.

In Kentucky, the women's central committee brought out the first issue of the *Heathen Helper*. Agnes Osborne, secretary of the committee, was also a competent journalist and had the financial backing of her brother, who was editor of the *Louisville Ledger*. The *Heathen Helper* gained quick popularity, cheered on by most state Baptist papers who were friends and supporters of the women's cause. One glaring exception was Kentucky's own *Western Recorder* and its very conservative editor, T. T. Eaton. In truth, the *Heathen Helper* gave his paper strong competition as it encouraged readers to organize meetings that eventually shaped WMU. Wives and daughters of many of the state Baptist papers editors were active in women's mission societies. These women wrote freely in the new *Heathen Helper* and addressed a readership clearly interested in organizing.

Various states reported ideas and progress, encouraging each other and working on the fine points of how to organize and operate. As a result, the women who wrote for the new publications organized a procession of meetings, which essentially led to the beginning of WMU.

The *Heathen Helper* consistently challenged women to deeper missions commitment, even as it challenged the status quo. In just its second issue, pioneer China missionary Martha Foster Crawford of Alabama wrote about the need for men and women to work together in mission support. She believed women's groups should work not only for women but also for the conversion of men. Along with Crawford, only one other missionary wife had actively been doing the work of a missionary, so her suggestion carried a lot of weight.

The preparatory work had begun. In 1883, the Southern Baptist Convention met in Waco, and Texas women went all out to welcome Baptist women to their state. A crowd of 3,000 Southern Baptists were hosted royally and given free lodging and meals. At least 700 of them were women, by far a record crowd. The women met in the Methodist church, and many of the men came to listen. There was an air of excitement as Sallie Rochester Ford presided. A famous writer and speaker, the beautiful Sallie Rochester Ford was a magnet.

Sallie Rochester Ford

Brilliant, beautiful Sallie Rochester Ford was said to be "one of God's good gifts to a lost world." Born in 1828 into a prominent Louisville family, Sallie Rochester graduated from a Georgetown, Kentucky, girls school in 1847 with highest honors. At the age of 27, she married a Louisville pastor who soon purchased a religious monthly paper. Sallie Ford began her writing career by helping produce each issue. After living in several cities, the Fords settled in St. Louis and the publication became *Ford's Christian Repository.* Much of its success was due to Sallie, who edited the paper's Home Department.

Sallie was also a well-known fiction writer of the time. Her most successful novel, *Grace Truman*, went to many reprints and was highly influential in promoting spiritual growth in its readers. Not only talented as a writer, Sallie's organizational skills were exceptional. She was the guiding light in the establishment of the Woman's Baptist Missionary Society in St. Louis. Then in 1877 she was one of the organizers of the Missouri Baptist Women's Foreign Missionary Society, the forerunner of the WMU of Missouri.

Sallie was a leading figure in organizing and articulating the birth of WMU. With ease and skill she presided over the informal women's sessions during the Southern Baptist Conventions in 1883, 1885, 1886, and 1887. She was too controversial a figure to become an elected national leader, but she brilliantly paved the way for those who did assume leadership.

Sallie Rochester Ford left the imprint of her faith and skill on generations to come.

From *Laborers Together with God* by Catherine Allen (WMU, 1987).

Sallie Ford introduced Martha Foster Crawford as speaker. This was a little uncomfortable for many people in the audience, for they were not accustomed to women speakers. J. A. Hackett, whose late wife had been on the *Heathen Helper*'s staff, diffused the uneasy feeling by standing up and saying: "Let every one keep very quiety [sic] now; this is the opportunity of our lives."[1]

Martha Crawford's presence was riveting. Onlookers said, "Her face lighted up like an angel's." Never before had a woman made a speech to a crowd of Baptist men and women. Martha Crawford had a missionary's sensitivity to culture. She relaxed the meeting by commenting that this was very informal, and she would speak generally about China and then answer questions. The crowd was fascinated and spontaneously took up an offering for her work in China.[2]

Martha Crawford's impact on both the women and men of China is evident even to this day. For years, she taught young men in the famous Monument Street Church in Tengchow, China. A stone memorial tablet honoring her effective and faithful ministry survived China's twentieth-century Cultural Revolution. That tablet still hangs on the church's wall, 100 years after her death, a silent tribute to her faithfulness in sharing the gospel.

The next day, Sallie Ford again convened the group. This day, men made speeches as well. Baltimore's First Baptist Church pastor urged the women to go home and organize societies. "Women are the ruling power in the world. Man is the head, woman is the neck. She turns the head any way she wants to." And this highly successful women's meeting became known as the meeting that "sent a thrill all through the South."[3]

The 1884 Southern Baptist Convention was in Baltimore. Ann Graves's daughter Lily wrote all the state central committees asking for a report, and thus the seedling of a national organization began to take root. Twelve states gave reports. By that time, the number of societies had increased to 642, and women's contributions were up by 68 percent.

At the Convention, young leader Joshua Levering (Annie Armstrong's cousin) proposed that the HMB employ a woman to help organize women's groups, and opponents objected. Then another young pastor accused the leaders of being "old fogies." By now, the Convention was polarized and the women did not press the issue. Instead, they prayed. Several women leaders covenanted to pray on the morning of the first Sunday of each month and appealed through the press for more women to join. Martha Crawford joined them in prayer from China.

Then came the 1885 meeting in Augusta, and tension mounted. Neither faction trusted the other; and in 1886 in Montgomery, the disagreements continued to be bitter. This tension over women's roles was affecting giving; and by 1887, women's contributions to the FMB had slipped by 33 percent.

Again, in 1887, Sallie Ford pulled the women together for the meeting in Louisville. Three hundred women came together with the intention of talking business. And, this year, men were excluded. The only special speaker was Anne Luther Bagby, then on furlough (now stateside assignment) as a missionary to Brazil. Some women felt they should select officers and an ongoing program at once, but Annie Armstrong and Martha McIntosh suggested they delay. These two pushed for an organization so finely tuned that it could not be destroyed. The women decided to carefully lay out their strategy for the 1888 meeting the coming year.

This statement of intent clearly declared that they had no desire "to interfere with the management of the existing Boards . . . either in the appointment of missionaries or in direction of mission work." And Annie

Armstrong's sister Alice flooded the papers with a series of educational articles on the history and vision of women's work for missions. Alice also laid down the bottom line: the mission boards need money, and women's organizations make money.

Thus, the stage was set for 1888 and the Richmond Convention. But not even the visionary Annie Armstrong, nor any of those committed women, foresaw what God had in mind for this organization just waiting to be born.

3
1888–1900

The official founding of Woman's Missionary Union was no hastily thrown together occasion. Decades of prayer, passion, and preparation preceded that historic founding day—May 14, 1888. In preparation, Baltimore's James Pollard had the year before proposed a harmless-sounding motion to the Southern Baptist Convention (SBC) calling for a committee to study ways the Convention might be improved. The committee chairman was Annie and Alice Armstrong's pastor, F. M. Ellis. All the men on this new committee were sympathetic to organized women's work, with one exception: T. T. Eaton of Kentucky's *Western Recorder.*

The women carefully prepared for their May meeting. Two excellent papers were presented by behind-the-scenes promoters Alice Armstrong and Fanny Coker Stout, the pastor's wife and closest friend of WMU's first president, Martha McIntosh. Presiding at the meeting was Mrs. Theodore Whitford, a young pastor's wife in Richmond and a huge supporter of women's missions. She was not a known figure who might arouse antagonism among the women on either side of contentious issues or on the part of Convention fathers.

There were 32 official delegates from 12 states. At least 200 women were known to be there, but the actual number was probably larger. One woman, Abby Manly Gwathmey, who later became national president, deliberately brought her 10-year-old twin daughters so they could see history in the making.

After the two vital papers were presented, the women decided to wait to take an official vote until after the SBC had expressed its opinion on the committee report. Meantime, they diligently worked out all the plans for a general organization.

The SBC meeting began on a rainy Friday morning, May 11. Ellis presented his report on needed Convention improvements, including a mild mention of women's work. Other issues were debated a full four hours. By this time, Convention delegates were anxious, not wanting to miss a reception at the governor's mansion. The entire committee report passed with no debate on women's matters.

Clearly, one of the big problems facing the SBC was funding for the boards. Ellis suggested two prophetic solutions: systematic, proportionate giving and approval of women's missionary societies. His sense was that an underutilized power in churches had been lying dormant—the power and influence of women. He referred to them as "the great power by which the gospel is to be sent to the ends of the earth."[1]

The message women gleaned from the Convention was: "Do as you please, only send your money." That following Monday morning the women sang "Rock of Ages"; Alice Armstrong spoke; Martha McIntosh called the women to prayer; then the women took a final vote, and the organization—Woman's Missionary Union—was officially born.

Quietly, powerful 40-year-old Martha McIntosh was selected as the first national president. McIntosh was indeed a proven champion of foreign missions. Annie Armstrong was chosen as corresponding secretary. This tall, attractive, dynamic young woman was a second-generation women's leader.

The first name given the new national organization was the Executive Committee of Woman's Mission Societies, Auxiliary to the Southern Baptist Convention.

Abby Manly Gwathmey: 1894–95

Abby Manly Gwathmey only served as national president for 1 year (as an interim while Fannie Heck was recovering from illness), but her impact continued throughout her fruitful life. Abby was the only president in the first 90 years of WMU to use her own name in preference to her husband's. Born in Alabama in 1839, Abby's father's name, Basil Manly, was synonymous with *Baptist*. He was vice-president of the Triennial Convention, a prominent pastor, president of the University of Alabama, and then pastor of First Baptist Church Montgomery. Abby was one of eight children, and several of her brothers were outstanding Baptist leaders as well. Her brother Basil Jr. was a founder of Southern Baptist Theological Seminary and the founding president of Richmond Female Institute. Basil soon brought his beautiful sister Abby to be educated in the college's first class.

Another of the college's founders was William Gwathmey, a wealthy bachelor and the son of a mother who was deeply involved in a Virginia missionary society. Abby was married to the 39-year-old doctor just after her 19th birthday and became the mother of nine children, several of whom were prominent Baptist leaders.

Abby lived a lifetime loving missions and serving in laying the foundation of WMU. William Gwathmey's wealth did not survive the Civil War, and after her husband's premature death, Abby supported her children on her own. She became a bookkeeper for the *Foreign Mission Journal* for several years, thus becoming the first officer of WMU ever to have been gainfully employed.

Throughout life, her missions heart clearly reverberated. Maybe sensing history in the making, she took her 10-year-old twins, Maria and Alberta, to the 1888 founding session of WMU. Abby was involved with WMU on every level from local, county, state, to national service. During her year as national president, the week of prayer and offering for home missions was born. Fannie Heck regained her health and returned to the presidency, but Abby Manly Gwathmey continued her devotion and involvement throughout her 78 years. Even a secular reporter noted her outstanding life, spirit, and contributions, concluding: "She is indeed a woman of great power."

From *Laborers Together with God* by Catherine Allen (WMU, 1987).

The name did not officially become WMU until 1890, in order to sound less threatening. The organizers had no wish to draw further criticism. The end result was doubt-less what naysayers had suspected it would be; under any name, this seemingly meek organization would alter Southern Baptist life.

From the vantage point of history, the actual founding of WMU was strikingly peaceful. By using the term *auxiliary*, the women were as close as they could get to the Convention without an invitation to be fully partici-pating members. McIntosh and Armstrong were appointed to confer with the mission boards, which gladly agreed to pay WMU's expenses in return for their contributions to missions.

The new group established Baltimore as headquarters, and included a library and publishing operation. The president/corresponding secretary arrangement foreshadowed WMU's later organization. The president became an elected officer, representing the states' volunteers. State committees developed structure and became liaisons between the general office and local churches. Previous committees only had the *Heathen Helper* and board secretaries to coordinate work; now they had general officers to write and give direction.

WMU leaders and the mission boards came to an agreement for funding the new organization. It was decided that funds raised by the new organization would go directly to the boards. The WMU officers would not receive pay, but the organization's expenses would be paid by the mission boards, with the FMB paying more than half, since they received more than half the benefits of the women's work.

On a Local Level

Women in local churches had clearly demonstrated their skill at raising funds, and they continued to get many requests for financial help, missions-related and otherwise. The national organization did not set limits on the states. Each church, association, and state was free to give and respond as they chose. Therefore, state WMU dollars built local colleges, established scholarships for young women, and operated social work institutions. Of course, funds at the national level went to the support of the two mission boards.

Local societies were intrigued by faraway projects suggested by Baltimore headquarters. Annie Armstrong was skilled at developing ventures that captured the women's interest. She led states in packing missionaries' necessity boxes and planting gardens, with the proceeds going to missions. She further inspired the women with literature that provided information and prayer promptings.

WMU Leaders Reach Out

Many of the early leaders were from prominent families and had more time to devote to leadership. Yet, from the very beginning, the national officers encouraged state WMUs to involve all women, even those who had more skills and dedication than money.

Since Annie Armstrong was from a family with secure financial resources, she never accepted a salary. The money that would have been used for her salary was poured into missions work. Later, as her own personal funds were declining, she did accept travel money so she could make necessary trips to further the ministry.

Diversity became a part of WMU. That very first year, WMU began its involvement with Spanish-speaking people in the US. Mina Everett had been a foreign (now international) missionary until health issues forced her to return to the US. She was appointed a missionary to

Martha McIntosh: 1888–92

 Her early years sounded like a chapter in an antebellum southern novel. Martha "Mattie" McIntosh was born in 1848 in a lovely southern mansion with verandas on three sides. As a little girl, she rode horses bareback on the wide green lawns and played beneath cool shade trees. The family's prosperous plantation flourished, even after her father died when Mattie was just 10 years old. Her capable mother managed the vast plantation's network of business. And her father's mother, Margaret McIntosh, reigned over the family kingdom. Each day the eight children went to their grandmother's room for Bible readings, and each Sunday she took them in the family carriage to Welsh Neck Baptist Church. Strong women set an early example for little Mattie.

Even the horrors of the war did not destroy the family, and much of their fortune survived. Little blue-eyed Martha grew up to be a tall and graceful young woman. She was, throughout life, a steward of God's manifold blessings.

One of her friends at church, Ellen Edwards, had a brother who was a missionary to China. Ellen brought home from Baltimore mite boxes for missions. The women were enthusiastic about helping support her brother, J. B. Hartwell. Then in 1872, John and Fanny Stout came to pastor the church and immediately organized a woman's missionary society. Martha and her sister Louise were charter members.

A vice-president at the Foreign Mission Board (FMB) wrote, asking Martha to serve on South Carolina's central committee. And that was the beginning. Fanny Stout was president and Martha the corresponding secretary and treasurer—writing prolifically to women around the state. Her signature, M. E. McIntosh, became a familiar sight. (The *E* stood for nothing; Martha simply felt she needed an initial.)

Martha McIntosh was a remarkable fund-raiser; and when in 1888 the Christmas offering was instigated at the urging of Lottie Moon, McIntosh's own state of South Carolina accounted for one-third of the total offering, which exceeded $3,000.

It was Martha who called the women to action in 1888, and she was wisely chosen as the first president of WMU. Fellow Baptists praised her for her wise, prayerful leadership, something she was able to do without sacrificing her "womanly dignity." Another leader observed that her "gentle, refined ways often masked unsuspected force and executive ability."

And, there was romance in her life. After serving as president of WMU for 4 years, she declined reelection. The reason became evident in 1895, when she married the widowed T. Percy Bell, head of the Sunday School Board in Nashville, Tennessee. Years before, Martha's new husband had wanted to go to China as a missionary, but church politics interfered. Now Martha became mother to Bell's son, Frank, and young daughters, Bertha and Ada. Within a year, the Bells moved to Atlanta, where he owned the influential *Christian Index*. Not surprisingly, Martha Bell was extremely active in Georgia WMU.

In 1914, Martha's stepdaughter Ada announced she was going to China as a missionary. Martha declared, "Ada, how can you leave me?" Ada replied, "Who was it who taught me to love missions? Who has told me stories about China ever since I was a little girl?"

Percy's health failed the next year, and he died in 1916. Ada invited her beloved stepmother to join her in China. In 1918, when she was 70 years old, Martha McIntosh Bell sailed alone for China. Ill health and precarious conditions forced the two women to leave in 1921, but Martha's dream of missions in China became reality. She assisted Ada in her station of Tengchow, the very city where Lottie Moon had served so long.

Martha died suddenly in 1922, but her legacy remained. Ada told of her cherished stepmother: "I know of no one else who explains the word *service* in all situations of life. So very rare, a consistent Christian all day, every day." Martha McIntosh Bell beautifully set a pattern for the WMU presidents who followed in her train.

Portions from *Laborers Together with God* by Catherine Allen (WMU, 1987).

Mexicans in San Antonio and raised funds from women to build the first US house of worship for Hispanics. At the same time, Everett served as secretary of Texas Baptist women and fostered their concern for Mexican neighbors.

By 1891, WMU members had already been shipping supplies to missionaries in Indian Territory for 9 years. That same year, a WMU organization was established among Native American Southern Baptist churches with their own central committee. WMU welcomed Indian

Territory in the union, and its vice-president was on the same basis as those from each state. (In 1896, two Native American women were delegates to the Annual Meeting, a historic first.)

In 1896, Marie Buhlmaier, herself an immigrant, was employed to assist WMU with migrant missions. Marie was paid through the Home Mission Board (HMB) with WMU-raised funds, with WMU supervising her work. Marie was the first home (now North American) missionary to do what was later considered Christian social ministries and the first woman to work with migrants. Buhlmaier and Armstrong had great admiration and respect for one another. And both were trailblazers.

Staffing and Funding the Work

The pioneer women of WMU drew up the first constitution in 1888 for a slate of officers headed by a president, corresponding secretary, recording secretary, and a treasurer. In addition, each state would nominate a vice-president to serve with the general officers.

WMU officers set out with the purpose of funding missions, and for more than 117 years have remained true to their original intent. During the first year of organization, they established the habit of victory. Lottie Moon had the magnetism to propose and inspire the first annual offering for foreign missions. And the very first year, Martha McIntosh distributed 4,300 missions offering envelopes in South Carolina alone. The just-born WMU set a daring goal of $2,000—and the final tally was $3,315.26. South Carolina led the states by contributing one-third of that total. Then in 1892, Lottie Moon herself appeared at the Annual Meeting and created a sensation. That same year, women first observed a week of prayer in conjunction with the offering. (To this day, the Lottie Moon Christmas Offering® remains the largest single missions offering endeavor in the world.)

In relation to home missions endeavors, only a thin line separated WMU and home missions careers. Martha "Mattie" Nelson did home missions work in New Orleans. In 1888, she became the first WMU worker in Mississippi, where she traveled and organized societies. Nelson is generally considered to be the first state missionary.[2] In 1891, Eliza Hyde was a city missionary in South Carolina. She was a strong promoter of Sunbeam Bands, especially among children who worked as mill hands.

Southern mountain folks were also included in ministry. In 1900, there were already volunteer teachers conducting summer schools. Fifty women went into North Carolina's mountains to teach. WMU's "box" program reached these isolated spots with food, clothes, and household necessities. Georgia and Virginia WMUs both funded schools for mountain girls.

> Annie Armstrong knew box work would attract women's interests. In 1890, she suggested boxed donations for frontier missionaries. Women made and shipped large boxes or barrels of food, clothes, books, and supplies to the frontier. One time the women learned that a woman missionary had walked six miles to borrow a single needle. Immediately, women prepared packs of needles, thread, and pins to put in the next boxes that they packed.
>
> Within 8 years of WMU's founding, more than 200 missionary families were being helped through the WMU box project. In that eighth year alone, the value of the boxes was over $21,000. That meant that an average box would raise a missionary's income by 25 percent. In those early days, the boxes proved a wonderful tool for educating societies about missionaries and their needs. They felt a personal involvement.

WMU leaders and members constantly opposed denominational debt, and knew they were not responsible for accruing the debts. In fact, they had no voice in debt decisions, yet they felt responsible for resolving the issue.

Some women believed that if they had only given more, the indebtedness would not have occurred.

In 1894, the FMB asked WMU to raise $5,000 toward their debt of $30,000. Armstrong immediately issued a leaflet, and state WMUs divided up the amount. When all was totaled, the women raised more than $5,000. The following year they again raised more than $5,000, this time for the HMB. Not surprisingly, debts continued to mount, and for decades women continued to pay the boards' debts. Those early, struggling years, thousands of individual women gave sacrificially and in turn inspired others to do the same.

Along with this special giving, WMU was also underwriting the costs of women missionaries. Actually, the women were providing the FMB with general funds, yet staying out of Board policy. All the while, WMU was providing partial support for women missionaries, and in 1892 they took on the support of all 54 women missionaries.

Reaching Beyond Class, Race, or Privilege

WMU provided more than finances to the boards. Baltimore women's work set a pattern for HMB social work ministries. They dotted their city with clubs and classes for immigrants, the poor, and African Americans with great needs. And Armstrong convinced the HMB to allocate $10 to $12 for each activity center.

The women worked hard to develop ways to meet the needs of individuals without endorsing the social gospel movement of the period, which proposed that the church seek to improve society in order to help people individually. On the contrary, Southern Baptists believed personal conversion would result in an improved society.

This societal trend did not deter women from extending help to the poorest and most helpless. Virginia Baptist women established a home for the aged in

Richmond, and in 1890, Georgia women began operating the Georgia Baptist Children's Home. Even 10 years earlier, Texas women were involved in helping orphans and elderly ministers.

Ministry to African Americans varied according to area. In 1892, the WMU plan of work incorporated principles of working cooperatively. WMU's approach was both "with and for," and included industrial schools for African American children and mothers' meetings for the women. Some of the best examples of working together with African American Baptists were in Baltimore. Armstrong and Maryland's Home Mission Society helped local African American women organize an orphanage.

Annie Armstrong tirelessly urged Southern Baptist women to organize efforts for African American women by producing multiple tracts promoting her ideas. Her guest authors included Mrs. V. W. Broughton, a leading African American Baptist woman, and Booker T. Washington, the legendary educator and scientist.

Annie Armstrong considered the race question and felt it was the personal responsibility of Southern Baptist women to minister to African Americans. Her urgent concern for Africa fostered her view of African Americans as potential missionaries. She was forward thinking beyond many of her era, believing there was great emerging leadership potential among African Americans.

WMU's first African American speaker at an Annual Meeting was in 1895. She addressed the body, declaring, "Nothing so good as the mothers' meetings had come to [us] since the emancipation."[3]

Armstrong was an insider in the development of the National Baptist Convention of black Baptists. When the Sunday School Board began assisting the National Baptist Publishing Board in Nashville in 1896, Armstrong was in the middle of the new venture.

In December 1896, L. G. Jordan, corresponding secretary of the National Baptist Foreign Mission Board, came to meet with Armstrong. Jordan brought his assistant—Nannie Helen Burroughs, who later became one of the most remarkable African American women in American history. Jordan, Burroughs, and Armstrong mapped out plans for a women's organization like WMU, and Armstrong and Burroughs visited African American churches to organize societies. Armstrong fully supported this burgeoning project by writing materials for Jordan's *Afro-American Herald.*

The resulting Women's Convention, Auxiliary to the National Baptist Convention, was officially born in Richmond in October 1900. It marked the beginning of a long-lasting relationship between the women's groups.

WMU's First Fight

In contrast with the SBC, known for everything from interpersonal disputes to name-calling, WMU's core relationships are a pool of tranquillity. However, a difference of opinion threatened the organization's progress early on. The unfortunate episodes involved brilliant, dedicated leaders, whose differences came close to stirring the tranquil waters of cooperation. These two leaders were Annie Armstrong and Fannie Heck.

In Heck's first term as president (1892–94), the two women worked together smoothly. In fact, Armstrong wanted Heck to be reelected in 1895. The next year, however, trouble brewed. The Sunday School Board established a Bible fund and Armstrong led WMU's promotion of it, although WMU had not formally voted to do so.

Heck objected, believing this fund would sap support from the mission boards. After the Annual Meeting, these two women left with different interpretations of what had been approved. It appears that Heck felt there needed to be some limits on Armstrong's decision-making powers. Furthermore, Heck wanted to participate in the work of the WMU Executive Committee, and Armstrong felt Heck's job was simply to preside at Annual Meetings. Armstrong would not even send her committee agendas to Heck.

The two women looked for supporters among the heads of the various boards. This was serious business to the Board secretaries, for their financial support and the peace of the Convention were at stake. The Board secretaries and the two WMU leaders met, and Heck and Armstrong agreed to keep their disagreements private. The two women avoided further contact before the 1899 Annual Meeting and honored their commitment not to air their differences.

It appears that Heck had agreed not to allow herself to be reelected. However, she delayed getting to the meeting, and thus permitted herself to be overwhelmingly reelected before declining the office. Heck returned to her home state of North Carolina and led the women with great skill. After Armstrong's resignation 6 years later, Heck again became national president.

With real wisdom, Armstrong and Heck did not publicize their disagreements, and the Board leaders maintained the privacy of the situation, thus preserving the integrity of Woman's Missionary Union. Their wisdom in doing so explains much about the succeeding character of WMU. The boards could have allowed WMU to dissolve over the situation, and the two women could have divided WMU by gaining public support from their individual areas. That they did not reveals volumes about the character and the enduring strength of the organization, as they placed WMU's interests above their private disputes.

The dual powers of WMU's president and chief executive officer were firmly determined. A true measure of discernment and diplomacy made a great difference in WMU's early success and ability to weather crises. In future decades, the women of WMU looked back in amazement at what God had done through them, as the flame of their passion for missions ignited new fires.

4
1901–1910

The beginning of the new century was, for the young Woman's Missionary Union, a time for establishing roots. They needed women who knew how to lead.

During the early 1900s, higher education of any kind for women was scarce. True theological education—seminary training—was mostly unavailable. A few married women attended classes at Southern Seminary with their husbands, but women who wanted diplomas or more thorough training had to go to the missionary training schools operated by Northern Baptist women in Chicago and Philadelphia.

A boost for the idea of training women came from E. Z. Simmons, who was furloughing from China in 1900. As the opportunity arose, he voiced his opinion concerning women missionaries: "When they come to China, they readily learn the language but they do not know how to teach the Bible, for they do not know it themselves. There should be a school for training women." He said northern training was not acceptable for southern ladies: "visiting the slums and other bad places without men as escorts . . . [and] loose doctrinal views."[1]

Simmons campaigned all over the country for a women's school. His idea was for Southern Seminary in Louisville to provide academic teaching with existing classes and credit privileges, and WMU to provide and staff a home for the single women as well as offer additional classes for females' concerns.

The dynamic missionary from China enlisted many supporters. The Sunday School Board saw the school as a way to strengthen Bible teaching. The Foreign Mission Board supported the idea, and Southern Seminary's president saw this as a solution to the awkwardness women students caused the seminary.

Simmons had his school fully planned and endorsed before he consulted WMU just weeks before the 1900 Annual Meeting. Annie Armstrong was approachable; but when she learned that a plan had already been developed and everyone automatically assumed WMU would undertake the project, she was clearly upset. She believed she should have been consulted earlier. But, personal issues aside, she knew that many people had previously opposed higher education for women, and she did not want WMU to handle this hot issue. Overall, she felt trapped in public disagreement with her traditional allies. WMU squelched the idea in 1900, but not even Annie Armstrong could stop the discussion.

Texas women pushed for a school; and in 1902, the Texas Baptist Women Mission Workers officers recruited a young woman's missionary society president to open one. Others also took action. The Louisville seminary in 1903 gave women official seats in the classrooms and for the first time allowed them to take examinations. A Dallas school opened in 1904 and the Maryland Baptist Union Association opened a women's training school in 1905.

Despite the alternatives, most Southern Baptists were convinced women should receive needed training in the proven classrooms of Louisville's Southern Seminary. In the 1903–4 term, 48 women enrolled, and proper housing and chaperoning became an immediate need. In 1904, Kentucky women sponsored a home for single women, with a local Baptist widow and her two young daughters moving in and providing single women with appropriate accommodations.

For some students the home was too expensive. Four single women, all foreign missions volunteers, rented an attic room near the school and ate bread and canned beans. W. O. Carver, the seminary professor who became the Grand Old Man of Missions, intervened. He convinced the young women that they should cooperate with the home to strengthen it for other students who would

Sarah Jessie Davis Stakely: 1899–1903

 Jessie Stakely holds a distinction held by no other national president; the 41-year-old Stakely had a baby while in office.

Jessie Davis was the daughter, granddaughter, and great-granddaughter of Baptist pastors. Born in 1861 in Georgia, she entered Southern Female College in 1879. Jessie was an outstanding student, musician, and debater. The nephew of the college president quickly took note of the beauty and talent of Jessie Davis. Charlie Stakely was 21 when they married and served as pastor of several churches in Georgia and South Carolina prior to becoming pastor of the influential First Baptist Church of Washington, D.C.

Jessie's missions interests were already well noted by this time, and she led their new church to be actively involved in WMU. By 1896, the District of Columbia was considered a state affiliate, and their first national vice-president was Jessie Davis Stakely. Three years later, 38-year-old Stakely was chosen as national president, and became an excellent and charming presider. Her husband accepted the pastorate of First Baptist Church, Montgomery, Alabama, but this did not deter Jessie from her duties as president.

After a tenure of 4 years, Jessie Stakely remained a WMU leader on all levels, including 8 years as national vice-president representing Alabama. One of her enduring contributions during this period of leadership was her nomination of the memorable Kathleen Mallory as secretary of Alabama WMU in 1910. She next supported Mallory's candidacy for secretary of Woman's Missionary Union, and the rest is history. Jessie Stakely's missions heart was evident to all who knew her. She urged women to work "with a desperate determination" to do their whole duty in fulfilling the Great Commission.

From *Laborers Together with God* by Catherine Allen (WMU, 1987).

Lillie Easterby Barker 1903–06

 Lillie Easterby Barker was another "first" among national WMU presidents—the first to have served as a foreign missionary. Born in Columbia, South Carolina, in 1865, she graduated from Chester Female Institute in 1887 and in 1888 married one of her professors, John A. Barker, a teacher and pastor. Both had felt the call to mission service and went to Brazil. Not a year later, Lillie nearly died of beriberi, and they were forced to return to America. Her missions heart never wavered, however, and after regaining strength, she became active in local, associational, and national WMU. Lillie was elected Virginia state WMU president in 1899, and in 1903 she was chosen as national president. On whatever level she served, Lillie Barker promoted the work of women in bringing in the kingdom of God. She later accepted the deanship of a Louisiana college, but before she could begin, developed breast cancer. Lillie Barker died in 1925, only 60 years old, but she had touched countless lives with her calm, grace, and courageous spiritual independence.

From *Laborers Together with God* by Catherine Allen (WMU, 1987).

come after them. He personally advanced a loan so the women could move into the ladies' home. In November 1904, the four moved in, and the home was established.

By February, the house was full, and a larger house was necessary. The boards recommended the home be supported by WMU. And knowing Armstrong and Barker, the corresponding secretary and president of WMU, were opposed to the Louisville program from the start, they wrote directly to state presidents (who made up the national board of vice-presidents). As a result, state presidents applied pressure, so much in fact that the presiding officer of the WMU headquarters Executive Committee resigned.

Armstrong took her anger to the 1905 Annual Meeting. Under her influence, the women voted against adopting the home by 25 to 22, but Barker and Armstrong knew they were losing the battle. The two announced they would not consent to reelection in 1906.

> In the early 1900s, WMU sought not to compete with existing publications, but to fill them with missions information. Annie Armstrong regularly wrote for Sunday School and young people's periodicals. Her sister Alice wrote and edited materials for children. As opportunity arose, the women included suggestions for meeting plans, Bible study, and prayer focused on missions. By 1906, they were producing leaflets for sale with the WMU imprint.
>
> *Our Mission Fields* was a quarterly magazine and the first official periodical of WMU. It began July 1906 with Fannie E. S. Heck as editor.

Despite the loss of national WMU leaders, individual states supported the school. Brochures about the Baptist Women's Missionary Training School and Home were sent to state WMU officers. The Louisville board of managers leased a large old mansion and cut rags for rugs for the arrival of unmarried women students.

WMU, in the midst of controversy and a changing society, saw a need and set out to meet it. Under a new slate of officers led by Fannie E. S. Heck, WMU opened the training school for women in 1907. Ultimately, the training school received a great deal of support. Some people considered the school WMU's greatest achievement.

Maud McLure was enlisted as the home's first principal. She was beautiful, regal, firm, cultured, and competent. McLure came from a long line of Southern Baptist leaders and was an accomplished musician. Steeped in a tradition of noblesse oblige, her life was dedicated to lift those less fortunate.

McLure joined in scrubbing the new building, and listened to Heck describe her high dreams for the school. The story goes that the night before the October 2, 1907, opening of the Woman's Missionary Union Training

School, McLure prayed to die before morning, knowing she would have to implement Heck's impossible dreams. The Lord did not answer that prayer, so McLure set out to create a school.

Unmarried women seminary students brought aprons and work dresses along with simple school clothes. They were assigned household chores to do three times daily. They even brought napkin rings to use for formal meals. The women excelled academically in this high-tone atmosphere. In the 1908 Old Testament class, all 14 women made grades of 90 or more, and three made 100. Out of 108 men, only 1 made 100.

The Woman's Missionary Union Training School was the child of WMU like no other cause. It presented the perfect opportunity to prepare women for public leadership. The principal of the school later became a member of the WMU Executive Committee and a frequent WMU speaker and writer. The school was featured in every WMU publication. Students graduated with intense loyalty to WMU and assumed leadership roles.

As WMU developed training courses and turned young women into leaders through the WMU Training School, they also encouraged state and associational officers to conduct institutes for training mission study teachers. This idea was based on the interdenominational mission study movement that was spreading rapidly among Southern Baptist women.

Praying Together

The need for women's spiritual training was illustrated by the problem of public prayer. Women of the early 1900s were often seen and not heard, especially in public. Clearly, a woman's role in church was limited according to the social standards of the day. Even though women were not permitted to do many things in church, they were expected to pray. However, prayer did not come easily to many women. They had seldom heard other women pray. The idea was something new to most Baptist women.

Initially, women of all ages were timid about leading in prayer. WMU literature encouraged praying together and reminded women of the Holy Spirit's ability to give strength in adversity. They were told to speak in simple, sincere terms, loudly enough for the group to hear. Nerve-racking as it might have been, prayer was always prescribed in outlines of missions meetings. And, with time, women grew more comfortable with praying aloud.

> Praying together for missions became a sturdy foundation block for WMU. Women asked at the Annual Meetings of 1905 and 1906 for a calendar of prayer similar to the one that the Woman's Mission Society of Augusta, Georgia, had printed and sold several years prior. The calendar listed names and stations of all missionaries and provided a guided plan for missions praying. The request was great, but so were publication costs. In 1906, several states guaranteed 2,000 sales, and the new WMU Literature Department agreed to publish a missionary calendar. The women devoured the whole supply, and 2,000 more were needed. The missionary calendar continued as a separate publication for 10 years and later became a monthly feature in the women's magazine. It became a hallmark of WMU's worldwide concern.

Almost from the beginning, WMU has observed days, weeks, or seasons of prayer. The first week of prayer associated with the Christmas offering for missions began in 1892 and quickly became tradition. In 1903, WMU began preparing material for young people to use in observing a week of prayer for the Christmas offering associated with Lottie Moon. And, women met together for a week in the spring to pray for home missions. In 1906 WMU encouraged each state to use the month of September to observe a season of prayer and offerings for missions work in their state.

Fannie E. S. Heck: 1892–94, 1906–15

 Fannie E. S. Heck stamped the imprint of her great mission spirit on WMU and her legacy has not faded with time. Born in Virginia during the Civil War, young Fannie grew up in a privileged home in Raleigh, North Carolina. A beautiful and accomplished young woman, Fannie had compelling dark eyes and a rich, full, and resonant voice. Her powers of persuasion made a lasting impact on Woman's Missionary Union. Fannie's mother loved missions passionately and passed on her dream of mission societies to her daughter. Fannie graduated from Hollins College in Virginia, as had Lottie Moon, one of her heroes.

Fannie Heck was a dynamic leader of multiple talents as organizer, writer, administrator, and charismatic speaker. She served longer than any other woman as president of national WMU, 15 years. For 9 additional years, she was North Carolina's state WMU president.

North Carolina women were not permitted to officially join the initial founding of WMU in 1888, but 25-year-old Fannie Heck was there for the meeting. She returned home, and along with co-workers in North Carolina, initiated a newspaper, *Missionary Talk.* This launched Fannie's literary career. She wrote two highly influential leaflets promoting missions, two books, and WMU's first full-length study book, *In Royal Service.*

During the time she was not national president, Fannie was involved in leading numerous philanthropic organizations. Because of disagreements with Annie Armstrong, she declined to continue as WMU president in 1899, but returned to the job in 1906, becoming one of the most influential women ever in the missions endeavors of Southern Baptists. For WMU's 25th anniversary celebration, the talented Heck wrote "The Woman's Hymn," which became WMU's permanent song.

Fannie Heck kept the ideal of sacrificial giving ever before women as she stated: "To have the privilege of giving is much; to have the privilege of giving *up* is more."

Fannie's broad thinking began to permeate the organization, and many of her ideals and goals have remained an integral part of WMU. She stressed religious devotion, prayer, mission study, and enlistment of women in mission service. Under her leadership, *Our Mission Fields,* the first WMU periodical, was born. This quarterly was the mother of *Royal Service,* which in turn preceded *Missions Mosaic.*

Fannie Heck had a charismatic speaking ability, and she made a lasting impression on thousands of women with her strong and resonant voice. Fannie's major address at the BWA Congress women's meeting in 1911 was powerful.

Suddenly, when she seemed at the pinnacle of her effectiveness, Fannie Heck was struck by intense pain. One Sunday morning, she managed to teach her class, then went home and to bed, never to be active on her feet again. Fannie offered her resignation as president in 1915. Likely, her illness was cancer. She took massive doses of medication to be able to endure the pain. Amazingly, no word of complaint ever left her room, and she somehow managed to write two books during those agonizing months.

No piece of literature is more remembered in WMU records than Fannie Heck's final message to the Union in 1915. She challenged her fellow women to pass on the passion of their missions vision. One of her pleas in that final address was that women "endeavor to see the needs of the world from God's standpoint."

This remarkable woman has been memorialized by numerous tributes and monuments. No doubt the one which would be most meaningful to her was the decision to name North Carolina's WMU missions offering for her. Nearly 100 years have passed, but the legacy of Fannie Heck has remained.

From *Laborers Together with God* by Catherine Allen (WMU, 1987).

WMU realized early on that prayer and action go hand in hand. As people learn about missions needs, they realize the importance of support through giving and prayer. Throughout the years, special missions offerings have been accompanied by intense times of prayer. And, those intense times of prayer have resulted in intercession for specific persons and situations of need.

A Place for Young Learners

From the very beginning, WMU encouraged children's missions bands. A regular smorgasbord of names for the young missions learners were tried, from Little Reapers to Rosebuds. George Braxton Taylor, son of missionaries to

Italy, found a children's Sunday School class that was called Sunbeams. Their teacher, Anna Elsom, came to be known as the Mother of Sunbeams. The two worked as a team; Taylor located missionary information and Elsom taught the little ones. Through Taylor's influence, Sunbeam Bands spread, and by 1889 there were more than 284 groups. With the encouragement of Taylor and the efforts of farsighted WMU leaders, in 1896, WMU took Sunbeams as their special task. Sunbeams had some amazing stories of raising money for missionaries and inspired the giving of their parents and churches.

Women had their societies and children had their bands, but there was a group that seemed to be left out of missions education. Young women needed to be involved; they needed their own organization. Upon Fannie Heck's return to the presidency also came a new organization. Young Woman's Auxiliary (YWA) was approved at the Annual Meeting of 1907. Heck saw YWA as a way to inform 16-to-25-year-old Baptist women about missions work and the opportunities for involvement through the Southern Baptist Convention.

Heck's vision for YWA was effective. Within 2 years there were 992 YWA organizations. By the end of the decade, Ann Hasseltine Judson college YWAs were flourishing as well.

On the other hand, young men presented a dilemma. For years, the women had pondered how to provide missions training for boys; after all, it was not proper for women to train young men. Heck, weighing the options, proposed forming the Order of Royal Ambassadors at the 1908 Annual Meeting. Women and boys followed her lead, and more than 100 chapters were organized the first year.

But there was still a missing link in missions for youth. WMU realized that preteen and young teenage girls were not receiving an opportunity to learn about and love missions. WMU began publishing literature in 1909 for

Edith Campbell Crane: 1907–12

The Crane family was well known among Texas Baptists, especially William Carey Crane, who was president of Baylor University. In 1907, a woman in the Crane family made Baptist history as well, when Edith Campbell Crane became the second corresponding secretary of Woman's Missionary Union.

Edith was born in Baltimore in 1876, and she and her three sisters all grew up to promote missions. One sister was a YWCA worker in China and another edited the WMU magazine for several years. Young Edith Crane graduated from Bryn Mawr among its ten top students. She was baptized at Eutaw Place Baptist Church, Annie Armstrong's home base. Longing to be a foreign missionary, she took a position with the YWCA, which was deeply involved in missions both at home and abroad. And then WMU called for her services.

Many new WMU efforts marked Edith's first years in office. Her style was in real contrast to Annie Armstrong's. Annie was activist, Edith contemplative. Annie was wary about working with non-Southern Baptists, whereas Edith loved interdenominational cooperation. Both were theologically conservative, however.

In less than five years, Edith Crane had traveled 50,000 miles and made hundreds of speeches. She was deeply involved with plans for the 1911 BWA meeting in Philadelphia, and she represented WMU at various conferences. The stress of vast responsibilities assumed by the dedicated and conscientious Edith led to her physical breakdown in 1911. Doctors ordered total rest and an extended leave. Her resignation was sadly accepted in January 1912.

Nearly a year later, and recovered from her illness, Edith Crane married a South Carolina lawyer she had met a year or so before. Firmly believing that husband and wife should belong to the same church and denomination, Edith Crane Lanham became a Methodist. Not surprisingly, Edith Lanham became the much-loved missionary society president in her new church—still involved in her call. She died when only 57, and at her memorial service her minister declared of Edith, "She has been my pastor."

From *Laborers Together with God* by Catherine Allen (WMU, 1987)

Junior Auxiliaries. YWAs were asked to foster the girls, and in the very next decade, GA (Girls' Auxiliary) was born.

Home Missions

WMU-sponsored home missions work expanded on several fronts during this decade. In 1901, WMU requested that the HMB approve female missionaries in the mines of Oklahoma. State WMU organizations and individuals gave money to support each appointee, and the idea was approved. Georgia and Virginia women supported two women missionaries working among Swedish miners, and other women were added to work in the ports of Norfolk and Galveston.

Mary C. Gambrell, who served as secretary of Texas Baptist women and as assistant to the secretary of the state mission board, developed a strong relationship with the Mexican people and the missionaries she supervised. She learned Spanish and fought for the social acceptance and education of Mexicans. She helped to organize the Texas Mexican Baptist Convention in 1910; however, she died before the new committee on women's work could report. She laid the foundation, but her work outlived her, as the WMU auxiliary to the Mexican Baptist Convention of Texas was established in 1917.[2]

Salaries, Trends, and Changing Times

In the formative years, WMU leaders gained experience in dealing with finance. The boards contributed to WMU's budget under the "recalling" system. WMU officers incurred or estimated expenses then "recalled" those expenses from the boards. Women were reluctant to request reimbursement, as they wanted as much money as possible to go to the missions fields.

In fact, WMU's first officers did not want to be paid at all. They could afford to give their services, and besides, society at that time viewed accepting a salary as unfeminine.

Working without pay, at a deficit so to speak, had several advantages. It gave the women a certain amount of underlying power over the mission boards' salaried officers, and it ensured more money for the support of missionaries on the field. The national office's example kept state WMU organizations from paying their workers also.

In 1900, the WMU Executive Committee considered paying Annie Armstrong, since she was contributing so much of her personal money to the operation of the organization. Nevertheless, she maintained her point of view and refused a salary; however, she did agree to accept travel money. This allowed her to spend more time, as much as half the year, on the field promoting missions work.

The boards attached a salary to Armstrong's job in 1903, although Armstrong refused the money. She vowed to resign from office if she were forced to accept pay. With wisdom, the leaders dropped the issue until her retirement in 1906, at which time her successor, Edith Campbell Crane, received a salary. The treasurer began receiving a small stipend in 1909, and between 1900 and 1912 almost every state WMU employed from one to three professional officers or staff.

In 1906, WMU leaders decided to publish literature for sale and use the profits to supplement the reimbursements they were receiving from the mission boards. The plan worked. Less money was needed from the boards, and WMU had taken its first step to becoming self-sufficient.

Facing New Challenges

The new century brought other changes, as women's interests expanded beyond farm and family. Under Heck's leadership WMU expanded its efforts beyond fund-raising and began focusing on mission study. In 1909, Heck set out to develop a program of personal service that focused on Southern Baptist principles.

With Heck at the helm, WMU faced two new needs: more office space and financial investment. As owner of the Woman's Missionary Union Training School, WMU was accumulating an endowment that needed to be invested for interest. The organization prudently used training school endowment funds to buy a building in Baltimore, then rent it to itself and to other tenants at an interest-earning rate. The first WMU-owned headquarters was dedicated on October 26, 1909.[3]

Woman's Missionary Union was expanding and growing in influence, eagerly anticipating challenges and opportunities that were rapidly unfolding. The nation was growing and changing, and WMU was determined to keep pace.

5
1911–1920

Early in the decade, WMU selected a new executive director whose tenure spanned four decades and contributed immeasurably to the stability and impact of Woman's Missionary Union through years of cataclysmic change in the nation and the world. Kathleen Mallory became director in 1912, and in her first 10 years, she and WMU were confronted with a number of challenges from society: women's right to vote, alcohol temperance, women joining the workforce, child labor, and World War I. And through it all, WMU leaders studied the Bible, prayed with intensity, evaluated the times, and moved forward in establishing a firm foundation for Southern Baptist missions.

Fannie Heck, WMU's charismatic president, spoke of WMU's ideals, including united prayer, Bible study, mission study, enlistment in mission service, giving, and training youth in missions. And before its 25th year, WMU had a full-blown program that would not appreciably change goals in the years that lay ahead.

It was Fannie Heck who spearheaded the joyous 25th anniversary celebration of WMU in 1913, writing WMU's first history, *In Royal Service*, in honor of the occasion. And it was in this decade that Kathleen Mallory compiled the first *Manual of WMU Methods*. It served, not as strict regulations, but as a guide for missions growth. Also during these years Girls' Auxiliary (GA) was organized. First called Junior Auxiliaries, the girls' groups were fostered by YWAs. The founding year was later claimed to be 1913, and its new name—Girls' Auxiliary—was bestowed in 1914. Camping for RAs and GAs was another first for the decade. Virginia Baptists introduced camping for RAs in 1917, and 2 years later, sponsored a GA camp as well.

Personal Service: WMU's Social Work

In 1909 the national office designed a plan for personal missions and social action, which they named "personal service." Instead of sending out two or three dozen women missionaries, WMU decided to "convert itself into a vast company of women who, by their leadership in it, feel called and appointed each in her own community to do such work." They acknowledged a spiritual duty to the "poor, neglected, and outcast of their own neighborhood."[1]

The personal service plan was a revolutionary idea that would take time to "grow up in the mind of the people," according to Fannie Heck. And, take time it did. Nearly 10 years later, fewer than 37 percent of the societies were participating in the plan.

Several barriers stood in the way of organized personal service. Many Southern Baptists believed a variety of adverse effects would result from the social gospel movement that emphasized community betterment (and sometimes what some people considered socialism) over individual salvation and holiness. Another barrier was Baptist independence, which typically worked against unified efforts. And yet another obstacle was finding time for local social missions when women were accustomed to the original agenda of mission support.

WMU published pamphlets, magazine articles, and other literature that outlined women's Christlike obligations to meet human need. And they tried a new approach. A leaflet on how to conduct a personal service survey was repeated throughout 1914 in the popular monthly women's magazine *Royal Service*. This leaflet encouraged women to conduct detailed surveys of their community to learn about the local economic and employment picture, sanitation levels, languages spoken, educational needs, and religious affiliations represented. The completed surveys raised awareness and led families to take corrective action as landowners, citizens, and employers.

As social science education and social work professions became popular, Southern Baptists became more open to personal service. By 1921 social work was a recognized method for Southern Baptist foreign missions, too.

As a young woman, Kate Waller Chambers served as an editor for the Southern Baptist publication the *Heathen Helper*. She stepped down from her position when she married, but missions remained an important part of her life. She donated money for WMU to establish a home where young missionary children could live while their parents were serving on the field. A suitable home, in Greenville, South Carolina, was named the Margaret Home, in honor of Kate's grandmother, mother, and daughter. Opened in 1905, it was a temporary home for 40 boys and girls and 15 furloughing missionaries. The home was no longer needed when conditions changed on the missions field and children were able to obtain an education while living with their parents. Subsequently, the Margaret Home was sold and the proceeds formed the basis of the Margaret Fund, a source for providing scholarships to missionary kids (MKs). The first scholarships were granted in 1916. The scholarship fund for MKs continues today, 90 years later.

The plight of the foreigner was a compelling force in personal service. Germans in Baltimore, Mexicans in Texas, and Cubans in Florida drew women's sympathies. WMU had particular sympathy for immigrant women, homebound and least likely of the family to learn English. Several ways were established to meet foreigners' needs, but good will centers and literacy lessons, which often resulted in permanent ethnic churches, were particularly effective.

Industrialization posed special concerns also. Women and children worked long hours for little pay in southern mines, factories, and mills. Many people who suffered from industrialization were displaced Baptists from rural churches. There were many aid techniques, but the most popular was to provide Woman's Missionary Societies and Sunbeam Bands convenient to workplaces.

Some WMU organizations ministered to people in their communities through skills workshops. The earliest Christian social work was the industrial school, requiring only a meeting place, teacher, and supplies. Classes on simple sewing, cooking, woodwork, and child-care skills were developed for children or adults. Mother's Clubs and Cheer-All Clubs for girls offered skill classes and included social teas, chats, and lectures concerning temperance, proper child rearing, and personal purity. Then in 1911 WMU began publishing the *Homemaker*, a manual for mothers' meetings and sewing schools.

Good Will Centers, WMU Training School, and Theological Education

In 1912, Maud McLure introduced the settlement house program to the Woman's Missionary Union Training School curriculum. The term *settlement house* was replaced by *good will center* in 1914 to demonstrate the good news of "peace on earth, good will to all men" (Luke 2:14). This program set the pace for local WMUs and provided students a missions laboratory. All training school students were required to practice their witness and ministry skills there.

McLure strictly supervised the school, spending a summer at the New York School of Philanthropy (later the School of Social Work) to study how it should be run.

Within 2 years, graduates of the Woman's Missionary Union Training School were directing settlements in Meridian, Norfolk, Atlanta, and Richmond. WMU expected good will centers to be operated and funded by volunteers. But when the training school began producing qualified social work professionals, WMU urged they be hired. The professional directors lived in the houses, earning a monthly salary of $40 to $50 to coordinate volunteer work.

During the first quarter of the century, women's enrollment in Baptist schools increased seven times, while enrollment of males only doubled. State WMUs raised large sums for endowments and dormitories, libraries and other needs, and fund-raising efforts continued even during the Depression.[2]

More Settlement House Work

One of the most remarkable settlement house workers was Agnes Osborne, editor of the *Heathen Helper*, and secretary pro tem for WMU's 1888 founding meeting. Born into a highly literate, progressive Christian family, she devoted her life to personal missions. By 1914 a doctor had joined her work in an industrial school in a needy section of Louisville. He conducted a mother and child clinic until Osborne opened a settlement house, where the doctor continued his clinic work. From 1916 until her death in 1930 she lived at the settlement house/center. A board of women from local churches paid the rent and operating costs. She received no salary.

A bequest from Southern Baptist Theological Seminary president James P. Boyce's estate purchased a building and Osborne's center became known as the James P. Boyce Settlement. Hundreds of Woman's Missionary Union Training School students worked with Osborne.

Another form of settlement was at the Sibley Mill in Augusta, Georgia. The mill furnished the house and the city's Baptists paid the salary of a 1915 Woman's Missionary Union Training School graduate. The settlement's services included a day nursery for mill women.

Good will centers were owned and operated by state and associational WMU organizations and sometimes by individual church WMUs. The centers resulted in thousands of conversions and the development of several new churches. Dozens of women gained professional ministry experience at the centers.[3]

Women and Other Seminaries

Meanwhile, Texas women still wanted a training school nearby. Even while the Woman's Missionary Union Training School was developing in Kentucky, the women of Texas ensured that they were included in the theological school that was forming at in Waco, Texas. It became Southwestern Baptist Theological Seminary in Fort Worth in 1910. Texas women sponsored a special building, and the Sunday School Board contributed to the cost. And, following Louisville's example, the Fort Worth Training School opened a good will center. By 1917 the Fort Worth Training School had one-third more students than Louisville. The school came under control of the SBC in 1923, with WMU assuming a fostering role that began 30 years of close kinship.

A women's training school was also central in the establishment of New Orleans Baptist Theological Seminary, first called Baptist Bible Institute. Women were admitted as students and were housed in their own dormitory. Within 6 years, almost half the students were women.

WMU also became involved in secondary education during this time, with several high schools offering missions outreach programs and mountain mission schools in Virginia and Georgia and a Louisiana French-speaking academy receiving funds from state WMU contributions.

Happily, WMU's focus on education has continued throughout the years. Scholarship funds, both state and national, have enabled women to pursue theological education and leadership development for generations.

Children's Work and Vacation Bible Schools

In another area of training, Fannie Heck took a great interest in developing programs for children. In 1912 there were 6,914 women's organizations and only 5,000 children's groups of assorted ages. Within a year, leaders had defined a structure for age-graded organizations and rounded out a full statement of purpose and program.

Another first for WMU occurred in 1914. The first known Daily Vacation Bible School under Southern Baptist auspices enrolled 102 children, taught by students at the Woman's Missionary Union Training School. Vacation Bible School (VBS) became a standard component of personal service, and within 5 years, 73 societies had conducted Vacation Bible Schools. Later on, the Sunday School Board appointed its first VBS staff member and promoted VBS as an activity for children within the church, whereas WMU had conducted VBS as missions outreach.[4]

Organizational Tools

WMU worked with the ladies aid societies found in many churches when they promoted the idea of "circle meetings" in 1917. Churches with large societies were encouraged to divide into groups or circles of women with similar interests. The circles were encouraged to have monthly meetings in addition to society meetings.

A comparatively new phenomenon was developing in America, and by the early 1900s, a number of women, either through economic necessity or by choice, were accepting jobs outside the home. This meant that they were not able to attend circle meetings during the daytime. For that reason, in 1914, WMU recommended that societies establish Business Women's Circles for women in their church who needed to meet at night.

WMU Elsewhere

WMU celebrated its 25th anniversary in 1913. That year's emphasis hymn sang of "sisters of many lands." It was truly a heartfelt sentiment, for WMU had indeed stretched its arms to include women in other countries. The oldest WMU abroad was formed in Brazil in 1908. Next came Cuba in 1913. Nigeria WMU and Mexico WMU were fully organized in 1919. And, Japan followed in 1920. As women of Cuba, Brazil, Nigeria, and China sent anniversary greetings to the organization they acknowledged as their mother in the faith, leaders began to think more about organizing WMU abroad.

In contrast, here at home, the early 1900s saw a slowdown in WMU affiliation. The Illinois State Association affiliated in 1911 and New Mexico WMU officially declared in 1912. Then westward expansion slowed for 30 years, as Southern and Northern Baptists reached an agreement not to encourage affiliates from outside their own region of the nation.[5]

The 25th anniversary marked the adoption of the WMU emblem. Emma Whitfield, a noted artist and historian, took the fish head, early sign of trust among Christians, and doubled it. Inside she pictured the open Bible, the torch of God's Spirit, and the world. On the Bible were the words, *Laborers Together with God. 1 Corinthians 3:9*. This became WMU's permanent watchword. For the 25th celebration, Fannie Heck wrote "The Woman's Hymn."

Teaching Missions

From the beginning, farsighted WMU officers knew they were making history and wanted to preserve it. They followed Heck's admonition to "think long thoughts. Plan not for the year but for the years." Heck was WMU's first major chronicler, writing the book-length history, *In Royal Service*, for WMU's 25th anniversary. Southern Baptist women studied the book in classes for 20 years.

In October 1914 the quarterly publication *Our Mission Fields* was replaced with a monthly magazine, *Royal Service*. The magazine, which drew 43,500 subscribers by 1920, initially included monthly meeting material for all ages and contained studies, missions news, WMU and denominational events. *Royal Service* set the standard among periodicals for excellence in missions material and inspiration.

Clearly the appetite for mission study was growing, and classes were held in connection with WMU Annual Meetings. State WMU organizations selected mission study chairmen or superintendents to organize massive classes. Virginia's Lillie Barker, former WMU president, crisscrossed her state, teaching mission study and WMU methods.

In 1918 WMU developed a prescribed course of study, including a reward system of certificates and seals. The keystone of the course was Kathleen Mallory's *Manual of WMU Methods,* accompanied by a biblical study of missions. *In Royal Service* covered missions history and more books offered studies on stewardship and contemporary Southern Baptist missions.

Urban Versus Rural: A Major Move

WMU was confronted with another challenge during the second decade of the century. America's population was shifting and WMU needed to plan accordingly to meet growing and changing needs. By this time, they had maintained a Baltimore-based headquarters for more than 30 years. In 1920, Georgia and Alabama representatives requested that the headquarters be moved closer to the organization's psychological hub. The proposal was so jarring that a decision was deferred.

Part of the motive to consider moving the head-quarters might have been the contrast between rural and urban lifestyles. Although the Baltimore women who first led WMU had a city mind-set and the early state commit-tees were in major cities, the vast majority of Southern Baptists and their churches were in rural areas.

The rural-urban differences eventually changed WMU's structure. Between 1895 and 1913, the rural ranks of WMU reorganized the state WMU organizations to be representative of each state, not just the cities. Establishing funds for officers' travel made this more feasible.

By 1914, two-thirds of Baptist churches were in rural areas and only one-eighth of them had missionary societies. WMU was an urban phenomenon. Rural WMU work was hindered because of irregular church activities, bad roads, antimissionary pastors and husbands, poor transportation, and women's reluctance to lead. The remedy came as offi-cers were enlisted at district and associational levels to work with country churches, while state officers secured free literature, prayer support, and mail contacts.

WMU and World War I

All this took place in the aftermath of a world war. The US entering World War I affected churches in countless ways. Many women personally felt the impact of husbands, sons, and brothers fighting for freedom. Personal service chairman Lulie Wharton put local WMUs in touch with their Red Cross chapters, and the women began to knit. Kathleen Mallory knitted everywhere she traveled until needles became second nature to her. By mid-1918 WMU women made 106,457 war relief articles.

Through the publications *Royal Service* and *Home and Foreign Fields,* WMU leaders urged women to conserve food. The HMB's representatives in US military camps asked WMU to place a service flag on each church pulpit to remind church members of the men and boys on the battlefront.

> Many WMU members who served as nurses or in other ways developed a working relationship with the Red Cross during World War I participated in the White Cross effort that continued after the war. *A Crusade of Compassion* was offered as a mission study book, and women were encouraged to prepare bandages, linens, and other supplies for Southern Baptist mission hospitals abroad. The White Cross combined the familiar personal service with box work and mission study. Before its end in the 1930s, White Cross work involved WMU in every state and assisted international and US Baptist hospitals.

One positive aspect of the war was that the men and boys who went overseas sent letters home describing foreign lands and people. More Southern Baptists than ever came to understand the need to send the Christian message to the far reaches of the world. In some ways that new awareness spurred the $75 Million Campaign, a courageous undertaking to provide funding to advance Baptist work on all fronts.

The $75 Million Campaign

Watching the women of WMU go about their work, the Southern Baptist agencies realized that the women had valuable skills when it came to raising money. In January 1919, the SBC's Education Commission asked WMU to help with a $15 million fund-raising drive. In exchange for moneys for several WMU projects, WMU agreed to raise $3 million for education and $1 million for the newly established Ministerial Relief and Annuity Board. The breathtaking truth was that WMU had only raised

$5 million dollars in its 30 years of existence. However, with great confidence, the women took on the challenge.

At the same time, the SBC needed $75 million to accomplish its plan to expand worldwide ministry. WMU's pledges to raise the other funds bolstered the courage of the men behind this bold education campaign to advance Baptist work. This was the first time SBC and state agencies had jointly planned and shared in a fund-raising drive. Without hesitation, Kathleen Mallory pledged WMU's cooperation.

By 1920, Kathleen Mallory and Minnie James were named to the Committee on Future Program, which carried out the campaign, marking this as the first time women were appointed to a non-WMU Convention committee. Woman's Missionary Union agreed to raise $15 million, a staggering sum for that era.

WMU officers went on the road to speak and to promote the campaign. Their strategy included organizers for each state, association, and church. WMU, which was already a good network of closely knit women, activated its existing organization, while the men promoting the general campaign had to recruit workers to raise money.

Early in WMU's history, women raised money to assist the Foreign and Home Mission Boards resolve debt. However, in 10 years the boards were in debt again. This time, concern over the FMB debt contributed to inescapable despair for several leaders. Lottie Moon knew of the mounting debt and stopped eating, eventually weakening her health and resulting in her death in 1912. The FMB's R. J. Willingham suffered such anxiety over its debt that he suffered a fatal breakdown in 1914. A plea was made at WMU's 1916 Annual Meeting, resulting in an extemporaneous offering exceeding $17,000.

The continuing debt situation spurred WMU's Emergency Women plan. Participants pledged to pay at least $5 in response to no more than one emergency appeal a year.

Minnie Lou Kennedy James: 1916–25

 Minnie Kennedy James is noted as the strongest advocate of denominational women's rights among the leaders of national WMU. Born in Texas in 1874, she was an Episcopalian until 4 years after her marriage. Lovely, blue-eyed Minnie, a gifted schoolteacher, married her principal when she was 20, he with the uniquely Baptist name of William Carey James. When W. C. entered the ministry, Minnie offered to change denominations; but W. C. turned her down, saying he wanted "no Baptist by convenience" in his church. She did indeed become a Baptist by conviction in 1898 and was immersed by her husband.

While serving a church in Kentucky, Minnie became officially involved in WMU work. After moving to Virginia, she became a state leader in WMU, revealing unique leadership skills. She exhibited great intellectual determination and poise, quickly becoming a protégée of Fannie Heck. It was Minnie James who engineered the plans for the memorable 25th anniversary celebration of WMU. She and Kathleen Mallory were the first WMU officers to sit at the conference table for business with the men of the SBC. Minnie quickly gained the reputation of one who "had the mind of a man and the emotions of a woman." She was one of the leaders in helping form the Cooperative Program, and later noted that as her greatest accomplishment. Minnie's years in the presidency led to increasing prestige and power for WMU.

She and her husband were a leadership duo in the SBC, he as executive secretary of the Southern Baptist Education Board, she as national WMU president. They were a mutually supportive team of great influence and courage. When the Board assumed control of the assembly grounds at Ridgecrest, North Carolina, WMU held its first convention-wide event there. Minnie also led on the international scene, presiding over women's meetings of the Baptist World Alliance in Stockholm in 1923.

Numerous responsibilities caused Minnie James to refuse reelection in 1925, but she continued to influence countless lives. She served many years as an emeritus leader and wrote regularly for *Royal Service.* Minnie James lived to be 89; and in her last year was lovingly cared for by WMU friends. She died in 1963. Most fittingly, the tombstone for Minnie and W. C. James reads: *Laborers Together with God.*

From *Laborers Together with God* by Catherine Allen (WMU, 1987)

WMU declared 9:00 A.M. every Monday as the campaign prayertime. WMU staff stopped their office work and housewives stopped their chores to pray. Prayer later proved more desperately needed than they thought when denominational agencies had second thoughts about sharing funds raised through the cooperative giving effort.

The first returns were extraordinary. At the end of 1919, Southern Baptists had pledged more than $92.6 million over 5 years. WMU for its part had pledged over $22 million. Based on these promises, SBC agencies borrowed money to expand, and sent out 84 missionaries and children for the Orient, the largest group ever sent by any mission board at one time.

As the pledges came in and the agencies became possessive, the $75 Million Campaign turned to disaster. Baptist agencies found fault with one another's methods of calculating and processing money. Eventually, the campaign organization disintegrated, and the agencies reverted to old, unilateral plans.

Yet throughout all the problems, including economic recession that hit the nation in 1920, WMU's cooperative network stood strong. In local churches women zealously kept count of their pledge progress. At Woodlawn Baptist Church in Birmingham, Alabama, the deacons decided to keep part of the WMU campaign money to pay a new church staff member's salary. The women rose up in righteous indignation. "The men know nothing about missions, not having made a study of it," the women noted. After pointed discussion, the men reversed their request and forwarded the total amount to campaign headquarters.

By the campaign's end in 1924, only 37.5 percent of Southern Baptists had made annual campaign contributions, with 16 percent of churches paying absolutely nothing. Still, the $75 Million Campaign constituted a turning point in giving and in expectations—the amount of money given and the number of people participating was notable.

The final tally showed Southern Baptists giving more than $58 million—78 percent of the goal and 64 percent of pledges. In contrast to the whole, WMU gave $15,025,000—100 percent of its quota and 67 percent of its pledge.

The $75 Million Campaign attracted more money in 5 years than the previous 74 years. It brought new influence for WMU. And the campaign was a prototype for the Cooperative Program, which was implemented in 1924.

Sadly, the agencies' reliance on pledges left them in deep debt for 20 years. The end wouldn't come until WMU again interceded during the next world war.

6
1921–1930

The 1920s brought new challenges to WMU. The proposal made in 1920 for Woman's Missionary Union headquarters to move away from Baltimore had caught some women by surprise, and the logistics seemed so overwhelming that the women decided to wait a year before making a decision.

When the proposal was back on the floor in 1921, the four cities still under consideration were Atlanta, Nashville, Birmingham, and Memphis. Nashville, home of the Sunday School Board, and Birmingham, then home of the Southern Baptist Convention (SBC) Education Board, received equal votes. The tiebreaking vote was cast by treasurer and young people's secretary, Juliette Mather. She said WMU would move to Birmingham, Alabama.

WMU headquarters set up operation at the 1111 Comer Building in downtown Birmingham in October 1921. The tallest building in the South at the time was WMU's home for 30 years. During that time, membership tripled, the publishing business soared, and staff grew.

Living in the Deep South

Birmingham was different from Baltimore. In the early 1920s, the mood of the South was becoming violent. Anglos and African Americans were becoming regular sparring partners. Stories of disgraceful treatment by Anglos toward African American women captured the attention of Woman's Missionary Union.

Early on, WMU had established a working relationship with African American women. And, seeing trouble brewing, they felt compelled to join forces with the Woman's Committee of the Commission on Interracial Cooperation, headquartered in Atlanta. The commission was formed to counter the growing violence in the South. Crucial points of cooperation included domestic service, child welfare, travel facilities, education, lynching, public press, and the right to vote. Both African American and Anglo women in the commission worked as equals. WMU named its personal service chairman, Annie Eubank, as its Woman's Committee representative. The Interracial Commission was endorsed in WMU's Plan of Work and personal service methods. And, WMU publications and programs included work with African Americans. Long before the SBC took notice, most state WMU organizations officially endorsed the commission and participated in forming state affiliates of the Woman's Committee.

"Soul-Winning" and Literacy

During this decade, personal evangelism was included in all WMU activities. Many of the earliest personal service techniques were clearly evangelistic activities. Cottage prayer meetings were usually conducted in the home of a non-Christian and appeared to be the best means of personal soul-winning. WMU members also visited in neighbors' homes, and even held services in which they led singing and gave Bible talks.

In this decade the emphasis on soul-winning merged with traditional tasks of personal service (sewing, providing food, nursing the sick) and proved to be a powerful combination. By 1926, WMU reported 4 million personal service visits, including many to explain the gospel.

Literacy was another natural outgrowth of personal service and witness. During the 1920s, WMU addressed the widespread problem of southern illiteracy, including literacy missions programs regularly in the WMU Plan of Work.

> WMU did not just support missionaries; it developed them. This reality did not become apparent to the denomination until the 1920s, when a disproportionate number of women applied to the Foreign Mission Board (FMB). In 1922 FMB secretary J. F. Love estimated that twice as many women as men were volunteering for missionary service. He attributed this phenomenon to "the influence of mothers, female teachers, WMU Mission Study Courses, and is an answer to prayers which go up daily to Him."[1]

Sing Around the Campfire

Camping has proven to be one of WMU's most effective and enduring methods of missions education. It was firmly established as a teaching tool by the 1920s. Kathleen Mallory spent most of her summers touring state encampments, leading a mission study conference or teaching about organizational methods.

Juliette Mather, national WMU's young people's secretary, dreamed of a camp for members of Young Woman's Auxiliary (YWA). Her idea became reality in 1924. This camp was the first regularly sponsored Baptist event at Ridgecrest Baptist Assembly (now LifeWay Conference Center at Ridgecrest), in Black Mountain, North Carolina. The YWA camp was held annually, except when prevented by wartime, through 1970, when YWA was discontinued in WMU's reorganization.

Missions Education and Age-Level Publications

World Comrades, a quarterly magazine for young people, began publication in October 1922. This was the first publication for children's missions education. Serving Sunbeams, Royal Ambassadors (RA), and Girls' Auxiliary (GA) members, it became so popular that it became a monthly publication in 2 years. Juliette Mather was the only editor of this magazine, which remained in existence for 31 years.[2]

Among her other duties as WMU's young people's secretary, Mather developed GA Forward Steps in 1928. Like the RA ranking system, Forward Steps gave individual recognition to girls who memorized assigned Scripture passages, studied denominational work, and completed other service requirements. As girls completed a step, they were awarded with recognition ceremonies called coronation services, which were often conducted on the associational level. Girls wore formal dresses and were crowned, caped, and given scepters and badges to mark their progression through the ranks. GAs' five ideals were based on WMU's purposes, or aims, which were articulated in the 1920s and included individual and united prayer, regular Bible and mission study, systematic and proportionate giving, and organized personal service.

Also in the 1920s a ranking system involving some 50 projects was developed for RA. They also had a badge and regalia.

In that same year, WMU gave $500 to Cuba WMU to launch *Nosotras*, a WMU magazine in Spanish. For 10 years, this magazine was the main item of literature used by Spanish-speaking women in the US.

Juliette Mather launched another magazine, *The Window of YWA*, in September 1929. Now young women aged 16 through 24 had their own missions magazine. Mather edited and wrote many articles in this monthly magazine.

Missions education began to expand not only for youth but among women as well. Business Women's Circles were organized in a number of churches in 1923, reaching out to provide for the growing number of women working outside the home.

The 1920s brought strong gains in the number of women in rural Baptist churches who participated in WMU. Actually, by 1926, 64 percent of WMU organizations were in rural churches. Nationwide, in 1929, WMU recorded more than a half million members.

Financially Speaking

Baptist leaders knew that whether the $75 Million Campaign failed or succeeded, they would have to work together to fund the denomination's work. At the 1923 WMU Annual Meeting, women discussed how to develop a plan for systematic and proportional giving by individuals and churches, the age-old dream of WMU. Meanwhile, the SBC appointed a Committee on Future Program. The result of the discussions was the Cooperative Program, which actually became the lifeline of Southern Baptist work.

WMU nurtured this program, helping birth it, feed it, protect it, tolerate it, and finally shape it into an instrument the women loved.

The general principles of the program were of unified giving by all church members to a central budget, with each church voluntarily forwarding a portion of its income to the state convention. Each state then forwarded a portion of its receipts to the SBC Executive Committee, who divided them among the various SBC agencies according to a predetermined scale. Although WMU agreed with those principles, it also insisted on preserving the right of designated giving. Through WMU's insistence, the 1925 guidelines said, "The special thank offerings for state and home missions and the Christmas Offering for Foreign Missions ingathered during the Week of Prayer of the Woman's Missionary Union for these respective causes shall be recognized as gifts in addition to the regular contributions to the Cooperative Program and shall not be subject to expense deduction or percentage bases."[3] Without this guarantee, WMU would never have promoted the Cooperative Program.

By this time, the Lottie Moon Christmas Offering was on its way to becoming a tradition. Back in 1918, Annie Armstrong had broken the silence of her retirement years to suggest the Christmas offering be named for its originator, Lottie Moon. However, in the 1920s, the offering was still often referred to as "the Christmas Offering for China." When the mission boards fell into jeopardizing debts, WMU looked around for offering inspiration. They found their most compelling tool to be the life story of Lottie Moon. Southern Baptists spent the week of prayer in January 1925 hearing about the tragic circumstances of Lottie's death from malnutrition and despair on Christmas Eve 1912. The effect was electrifying. The next offering increased 629 percent. By 1927 Una Roberts Lawrence had written a full-length biography of Lottie Moon. It would stay in print until 1980, when *The New Lottie Moon Story*, by Catherine Allen, was released.

> When the Home Mission Board (HMB) began to focus on mission study, they hired Una Roberts Lawrence as mission study editor. She was a prolific writer and an expert on missions. She wrote a full-length biography of Lottie Moon, ten mission study books, and numerous articles for magazines and pamphlets. Her biography of Lottie Moon, which was published by the Sunday School Board, remained in print for more than 50 years. Later, remaining on the HMB staff, she served also as WMU's volunteer mission study chairman.

Crises changed the 1927 Christmas offering. As the FMB debt continued to grow, it was discovered that the Board's treasurer had embezzled $103,772. (The HMB had suffered the same fate.) Even more alarming, the FMB announced that, as a result of the shortages, it would soon have to call its missionaries home. Not surprisingly, WMU decided to take drastic action.

Mallory led the way at the 1927 Annual Meeting. The women designated the first $48,000 of the next offering to pay for the return of 40 missionaries to their fields. WMU would guarantee their salaries for the years ahead.

The 1928 offering coincided with WMU's 40th anniversary emphasis on giving. WMU set a promotional theme, Christmas for Christ, and issued a theme poster for the first time. The women thought that debt retirement had lost its appeal to givers. They wanted a livelier goal and proposed to the FMB that they restrict part of the 1928 offering for sending 20 new missionaries to the field. WMU would aid in the selection, with priority given to graduates of the Woman's Missionary Union Training School. After four months of negotiation, the Board agreed to WMU's proposition.

The 1929 offering returned 60 foreign missionaries to their fields.

HMB Debt and Depression

The Home Mission Board's financial plight became critical in 1928, when long-term embezzlements by the Board's treasurer came to light. Stumbling under a debt of $2 million and a muddled reputation, the Board faced extinction. In January of the following year, the WMU Executive Committee lodged a formal request that every penny of that year's home missions offering be spent on missionary support. WMU thus restricted the money from being used to pay off the nervous and clamoring creditors. This plan demonstrated to persons inside and outside the denomination that Baptists would stand by the HMB, no matter what. Additionally, this far-reaching plan not only guaranteed the HMB's survival of the theft, but also the Board's survival during the Great Depression.

Kathleen Mallory: 1912–48

 Called "a Christian world citizen" and "the sweetheart of Alabama Baptists," Kathleen Mallory was the longest-serving executive director in the history of Woman's Missionary Union. She was petite and deceptively dainty, but under the gracious exterior there was a human dynamo with a passion for the world. That passion remained undiminished through an unprecedented 36 years at the helm of WMU.

Kathleen Mallory was born in Selma, Alabama, in 1879. Her father was a lawyer, Selma's mayor, and for a period of years, president of the Alabama Baptist Convention. Her mother was a staunch member of Woman's Missionary Society.

Kathleen graduated from Goucher College in Baltimore and became engaged the same year to Janney Lupton, a handsome young medical student at Johns Hopkins. They waited to marry until he had set up a practice, but Janney tragically died of tuberculosis in 1907. Kathleen was 28, and the direction of her life completely changed.

In 1909 Kathleen's father invited her to attend the state Baptist convention and read a missionary's letter to the WMU group meeting there. That letter from China unfolded her heart to missions.

In short order, 33-year-old Kathleen Mallory was chosen national WMU corresponding secretary (now called executive director). When first presented to WMU as their new leader, she immediately knelt before the assembled body to pray God's blessings on the years ahead. Humbly kneeling in prayer was a pattern she always followed; she frequently had hundreds of women praying in the same manner.

Kathleen Mallory became one of the best-known and most beloved names in Southern Baptist history. She traveled, spoke, and guided the women of SBC and concurrently edited *Royal Service.* And it was she who wrote the first full-length *Manual of WMU Methods.*

A woman of awesome self-discipline, she believed literally that gifts should be "fragrant with self-denial" and spent her 36 years in office living very simply. Kathleen Mallory never accepted a salary larger than that of a missionary, and on two extended trips to missions fields, in China and in South America, she insisted on paying the expenses herself.

Kathleen Mallory's motto was Fidelity to the Finish. In

January 1929, she proposed, in regard to the Annie Armstrong offering, that every penny go to missionary support and none be siphoned off for other needs. This was later hailed as one of the most far-reaching, constructive, and statesmanlike achievements in WMU history. The Great Depression hit, and because of Mallory's proposal, the survival of the HMB was guaranteed during the Depression.

Retiring at age 69, she had boosted Woman's Missionary Union to a position of quiet power. Her life and WMU's history became one and the same—inseparable. Kathleen Mallory's compassion for the world never changed. Thousands remembered her as the little woman who knelt in prayer, speaking to God as a child would speak to her father. Her memory remains a testimony to the love of the Lord she served so faithfully.

Portions from *Laborers Together with God* by Catherine Allen (WMU, 1987).

Women found other ways to help the HMB too. Although frontier box work had declined for two decades, the Depression revived those efforts. Box gifts were a way to give to home missions when there wasn't money to send. Women again packed whatever they could spare—cloth, needles, thread, food, and other supplies—and sent them to home missions fields. By 1930, as desperate need swept the country, box value reached $124,448, a 50 percent increase over 1928. Those offerings indicate both the need and the compassion of the era.

The decade of the 1920s ended with America facing the most colossal financial collapse in its history. WMU, like every organization, was faced with a challenge it could never have imagined, and which threatened its very existence. But challenge was not new to this stalwart band of Baptist women who determined to prevail, even in the face of such odds.

Ethlene Boone Cox: President 1925-33, Treasurer 1934-52

One of a kind describes Ethlene Boone Cox, a direct descendant of Daniel Boone. She was born in Tennessee in 1890 and became a Baptist after her marriage in Memphis to Wiley Jones Cox. Ethlene was soon involved in and committed to WMU, speaking frequently in the Tennessee area. When she spoke at her first state meeting, the women were awed by her charm and grace. In short order, she moved from state president to president of the national organization in 1925.

Ethlene Cox was an able president; however, it was her speaking ability that repeatedly awed and inspired any audience to whom she spoke. Her inner and outer beauty were both readily apparent to all audiences. She even spoke persuasively in the men's arena. In 1929, she became the first woman to address the Southern Baptist Convention. And, on another notable occasion, Ethlene was on the platform with Baptist statesman George W. Truett, president of the Baptist World Alliance. Truett was regarded as the outstanding preacher and orator of his era. He presided over the 1939 BWA meeting in Atlanta, when she was a featured speaker. The audience was so captivated by her clear, musical, compelling voice that she was widely considered Truett's oratorical match, no mean feat.

Not only was she an inspirational leader, Ethlene Cox was also a workhorse. She guided WMU in nursing the Cooperative Program in its infancy. With uncanny skill, she kept WMU solvent through the Great Depression, and was one of the first women to be named to the Baptist World Alliance Executive Committee.

Her husband's serious heart condition forced her resignation as president, but God had more in mind for the remarkable Ethlene Cox. She became the first salaried WMU treasurer. Thus she could work from home and at the same time continue as a top WMU official, lending both expertise and guidance to the organization that responded so willingly to her inspired leadership.

Ethlene Cox served as treasurer for an unprecedented 18 years, and in spite of various difficult physical problems, continued her job, a heavy speaking schedule, and regular writing. She was a magnet that drew the various leadership elements of national WMU together—pulling the best out of each one and serving to blend them in guiding WMU through some of its highest hours.

Ethlene Boone Cox died in 1965, at age 75. How fitting that the last Bible reading of this unique woman came from Psalm 66: "I cried unto Him with my mouth; he was extolled with my tongue." For more than four decades, the golden voice and servant heart of Ethlene Cox had given glory and praise to the God she served so magnificently.

Portions from *Laborers Together with God* by Catherine Allen (WMU, 1987).

7
1931–1940

A giant specter loomed over the whole nation during the decade of the 1930s—the Great Depression. No one was left unscathed, no organization untouched. Woman's Missionary Union was blessed with wise, capable, godly leadership, who worked as a team to keep WMU centered on its overarching aim, Depression notwithstanding. Kathleen Mallory, Ethlene Cox (first full-time treasurer of WMU following her tenure as president), and Laura Dell Armstrong were a formidable trio, combining compassion, skill, common sense, and sheer grit in overcoming great odds during a painful period for the entire nation.

Throughout the Depression, WMU sounded a note of optimism, keeping Annual Meetings upbeat. The WMU hymn chosen for the year 1931–32 flew in the face of the Depression's despair: "Joy to the World! The Lord Is Come."

By 1932 the Depression weighed heavily on the mission boards, and they were sinking deeper and deeper into debt. WMU, as usual, promised to "enter heartily" into SBC plans regarding debt. Despite the burden of family and nationwide economic struggle (unemployment reached a staggering 25 percent), WMU members were responsible for guaranteeing the support of 100 foreign missionaries through the Lottie Moon Christmas Offering. In fact, when all the giving was tallied at year's end, the WMU offerings made up 70 percent of the Foreign Mission Board's income.

The same trend continued each year, with WMU's financial contributions being absolutely essential to the survival of the boards. By 1934, WMU membership made up only 13.3 percent of total SBC membership, yet this small minority was supporting the majority of the work. In 1931, WMU gave approximately 70 percent of the mission board receipts.

Of course, influence went along with the money, and WMU leadership began having significant impact on field policy, something that raised objections from members of several boards. The proportion of single women on the field grew, and strong women's work grew in China, Brazil, Nigeria, and throughout Europe.

WMU's experience showed that increased giving came because of specific designations. The more specific the designation, the more the giving. Remembering how naming the Christmas offering for Lottie Moon had spurred its growth, WMU wanted to develop new incentive to giving for home missions. Consequently, in 1934 the annual home missions offering was named for Annie Armstrong. It worked. The first Annie Armstrong Offering reversed the falling trend in home missions giving and put 36 new missionaries on the field.

Nonetheless, the Great Depression cast a general pall over giving. By 1935, the mission boards owed nearly $3 million. However, thanks to WMU's foresight, missionaries continued to receive their salaries. From the beginning, WMU had always insisted that their dollars be used for missions, not for debts. This didn't mean that women didn't help reduce the debt, however. Without Woman's Missionary Union, the two mission boards would likely not have survived.

The stress of the Depression wore thin, and people across the nation began pulling their money out of banks. In 1933, the banks crashed and many people lost their savings. Subsequently, the assets of many WMU women did not survive. But somehow, funds came in, and yet again, the Home Mission Board (HMB) was saved. One sustaining force in Woman's Missionary Union was stressing the tithe. Thus, women led the way in giving and consequently increased their influence on Board policies.

Despite the Depression, WMU women believed in a tithe. WMU literature for all ages had given practical guidance on why and how to tithe. Women were taught they had access to money, whether or not they received a salary, and were responsible for tithing. Eggs and jars of jelly could be counted, with one in ten set aside for sale and church.

If a husband resisted tithing the family income, the wife could earn an amount equal to a proper tithe by selling her own products, then giving the proceeds to the church. If the family income had not been tithed, then the woman was at least responsible for tithing the household allowance that she managed. If a woman would adjust her spending to fit nine-tenths, women reasoned, surely the husband would permit one-tenth to go to the church.

Women were inspired to give with tithing songs and sayings. Popular jingles included "When Baptists All Learn How to Tithe" and "Jesus Wants Me for a Tither." Alma Wright delivered a classic address on tithing that was later distributed in 60,000 Sunday School Board tracts. Among her most quoted sayings was, "You can't take it with you, but you can send it on ahead."

As SBC debts mounted—up to $6 million by 1933—creativity was call to action. The SBC adopted the Hundred Thousand Club, an initiative in which 100,000 persons would pledge an extra $1 a month to pay off agency debts. WMU cooperated. By the end of the decade, Mallory printed on WMU's letterhead: *For a Debtless Denomination by 1945.*

The two boards had great confidence in WMU standing by its word. After Kathleen Mallory's assurance that WMU would not fail in giving, Foreign Mission Board (FMB) secretary M. Theron Rankin declared: "We will have our debts paid by 1945. WMU has promised

Laura Dell Malotte Armstrong: 1933–45

Laura Dell Malotte Armstrong added to the lists of "the only" and "the first" among Baptist women in America. Born in Missouri, Laura Malotte finished college and taught school before marrying attorney Frank Armstrong in 1907. Missouri Baptists required that some members of their state executive board be women, and Laura Armstrong honed her fine administrative skills in this select group, serving from 1919 to 1936. Then in 1920 she was asked to develop a missions-oriented student-work program on Missouri campuses. Speaking at the WMU Annual Meeting in Kansas City in 1923, Laura came to the attention of national leaders. Some people thought she was an unlikely leader. When she talked beyond her appointed three minutes, the timekeeper rang the bell, and she sat down suddenly, with sentence half finished. The audience laughed. Laura blushed. However, Kathleen Mallory and Ethlene Cox recognized her potential. She became Missouri WMU president in 1924 and was selected as national president in 1933.

Although Laura Armstrong was extraordinarily prepared for the presidency, she never became an impressive speaker compared to WMU's previous orators. Her thoughtful words were delivered in a halting manner. Nevertheless, Laura Armstrong led WMU with great skill for 12 years, launching formal stewardship education and a tithing emphasis. She put real emphasis on interracial cooperation, making it a priority. Laura was the first WMU president from west of the Mississippi River. And, another first, she was one of the first two women to serve on the influential SBC Executive Committee.

Laura Armstrong became president when America was deep in the Great Depression. However, with tenacious efficiency, all debts were paid during her tenure. She was a skilled fund-raiser and contributed greatly to the success of the WMU Training School in Louisville.

Laura was also involved in the Baptist World Alliance, presiding over BWA women's meetings in 1934 and 1939. By 1939, she was active on the Relief Committee of the Baptist World Alliance, pulling WMU support into European war relief efforts. She led resolutely as WMU met the challenges of wartime missions.

Throughout her term, Laura gained a reputation as a judicious leader, no doubt aided by her years of clerking in her husband's probate judge's office. She was calm, even-handed, always in charge in a gracious way.

High blood pressure affected Laura in 1937, and her massive workload took its toll. In 1945, she let other WMU leaders know she must retire, but the Annual Meeting could not be held that year. Just one week after she should have been relieved of all pressure, she died of a cerebral hemorrhage. Laura Armstrong was only 59. The obituary tribute from the Foreign Mission Board (FMB) spoke to her wisdom and courage, concluding: "She counted not her life dear unto herself."

Laura Armstrong was memorialized by those she loved. A training school was built in her name in Rome, Italy. A seminary was built and named for her in Havana, Cuba. Kathleen Mallory and others pointed to her diverse missions efforts as a worthy example. Her work would be remembered for generations.

From *Laborers Together with God* by Catherine Allen (WMU, 1987).

and you can count on them." And, true to form, when all the figures were tallied, Woman's Missionary Union had given over 60 percent of all debt payment money.

Segregation and the 1930s

Everyone in America was affected by the miseries of the Depression, but none more than African Americans. Early in the 1930s, WMU personal service chairman Una Lawrence renewed WMU's communication with Nannie Helen Burroughs that had begun when she and Annie Armstrong visited African American churches to organize societies. Burroughs was now a highly respected leader in the National Baptist Convention (NBC). Lawrence knew her through the Interracial Commission, but Kathleen Mallory had never met her. In 1932, national president Ethlene Cox appointed a committee to recommend the direction WMU should take on relationships with National Baptist women. Lawrence was appointed the official representative to the National Baptist Woman's Convention of 1932, and for nearly two decades a WMU representative was invited to the meeting.

A partnership developed, and the African American women began publishing the *Worker* in 1934, with Burroughs as the editor and Lawrence as a "special contributor." Burroughs became a popular speaker for WMU over a period of many years.

African American women also spoke frequently at WMU Annual Meetings. What dreadful irony that local ordinances usually demanded segregated seating. The close friendship of Nannie Helen Burroughs, WMU secretary Blanche White, and Una Lawrence was remarkable for America in the 1930s. Kathleen Mallory had never had such a friendship across racial lines, but that soon changed and she determined to work more closely with African Americans. Sometimes just the mechanics of breaking through the strict racial ordinances of the times were daunting.

At first, Mallory had difficulty in adjusting a lifetime of thought patterns and prejudice. After a gaffe or so in referring to her sisters of another race, she quickly learned and developed lasting ties of friendship. After one potentially slighting reference by Mallory, of which she was completely unaware, Lawrence and Burroughs took pains to prevent it getting into print. Lawrence apologized to Burroughs. And, with great dignity, Burroughs replied: "This shows how badly we need contact. Poor Miss Mallory doesn't know. . . . I'm glad you told me. We can help the dear soul and she will never know it." The experience actually proved a decisive one for Kathleen Mallory. She developed skills in the diplomacy of race relations, and Nannie Helen Burroughs came to adore her. Burroughs later said, "Miss Mallory is God's gift to us in this program of Christian service. Her soul is enlisted. She is genuinely sincere and far ahead in her thinking and desire."

One of WMU's 50th anniversary projects in 1938 was raising $10,000 for a fund to develop work with African

American women and children. In the way money always operates, trouble developed over who would handle the funds. NBC leaders wanted control; and then the Home Mission Board (HMB) agreed with the men of the NBC, considering that African American ministry was the turf of the HMB, not the women. The women, however, insisted that they weren't doing African American missions work but merely "woman's work with women," as usual.

The NBC even repudiated its ties with Burroughs, but WMU supported her and her work and leadership. Women established the Golden Jubilee Fund and used the funds to sponsor interracial institutes. Their purpose: to train African American women as leaders of missionary societies in their own churches.

The logistics for such organizations in the 1930s were nearly overwhelming, but WMU persisted, and leaders of both groups showed extraordinary commitment to the task. The heroism of Nannie Helen Burroughs was remarkable. Her heart and spirit were singular, and her influence widespread. A notable and beneficial characteristic was Burroughs's ability to overlook slights. She once told Lawrence, "I love your race a great deal more than they love mine." Her perseverance and dignity in the face of prejudice and bigotry were an example of the largeness of her heart and her love for Christ and His mission.

Mission Study

Institutes conducted across racial lines were only one of the major projects in the decade. Mission study flourished as well. In 1930, a committee of leaders from the various boards proposed a Church School of Missions. For the first time, men were getting involved in mission study. By 1937, WMU was encouraging churches in an association to undertake simultaneous Schools of Missions, bringing in missionaries to speak and inspire.

In other denominations, this kind of mission study was declining, but not among Southern Baptists. The WMU course of mission study was multilevel by 1933. Women could choose from 30 books, ranging from the study of missions in a particular country or area to biography or soul-winning. Credit was given for completed studies, based on WMU's Standard of Excellence, and certificates of award were issued from national headquarters.

Emma Leachman, a Home Mission Board field worker, was a popular mission study teacher. She conducted hundreds of studies and traveled many miles in the 1930s. Most of her studies were five classes of 50 minutes each. One of her classes was attended by more than 1,000 YWA members.

WMU's First Jubilee

By WMU's Jubilee (50th year), membership had grown more than 1,579 percent! Total membership grew from 37,200 in 1891 to 705,399 in 1938. (By comparison, Sunday School, also newly promoted, increased only 476 percent.) One spur to WMU's unprecedented growth was the well-developed network of leaders in tightly knit state and associational organizations.

Leadership was surely a key to WMU's growth and success. By the end of the 1930s, a different kind of WMU leadership had developed—one with education credentials. Courses in WMU work were taught at the WMU Training School in Louisville and other women's training schools related to seminaries.

Leadership also came from other directions. Business Women's Circles became prominent during this decade. These groups normally met in the evenings and tended to be independent. *Royal Service* published regular articles promoting and encouraging the groups.

Usually a WMU group grew in an established church, but sometimes the reverse was true. In 1933, Omer Shermer Alford (later president of Georgia WMU) and her husband, a textile engineer, moved to a mill village in Covington, Georgia. They discovered there was no Baptist church in the village, so Alford organized a women's prayer group. Initially, they stressed literacy, then organized a girls club that became a young woman's missionary society. A Woman's Missionary Society quickly followed. The next decade, a full-fledged church emerged from the WMU beginnings. And, true to form, the church dedicated its own building debt free.

In ethnic outreach, Hattie G. Pierson, in 1931, became the first field worker devoted to Hispanic women's work. She was followed by more women, both Hispanic and Anglo, who translated and published literature. All this activity was funded by WMU, and appropriated from the Annie Armstrong Offering.

The 1940 Annual Meeting was framed in an uneasy atmosphere; war was brewing in Europe and Asia and uncertainly influenced morale throughout the nation. A speaker at the meeting warned the women that their sons might be at the battlefront in a matter of months. The words were prophetic.

The SBC reached out that year of 1940 to Baptists around the world by appointing a Baptist World Emergency Committee. Included on that committee were WMU leaders Kathleen Mallory, Laura Dell Armstrong, and Blanche White. WMU responded to emergency financial appeals, providing support for British Baptist missionaries, bringing missionaries home from the Orient, and supporting HMB work among US military camps.

The women of WMU, along with the rest of America, had no idea what to expect in such a precarious and unstable time, but they were determined to face whatever might lie ahead with undaunted faith in the One they served.

8
1941–1950

America entered the new decade poised on the brink of war. Woman's Missionary Union began the 1940s with seasoned leadership. Executive director Kathleen Mallory had guided WMU through the upheavals of World War I and now was faced with a world conflict of cataclysmic proportions, one which would last 4 seemingly endless years. WMU records do not deal with the war as an issue in itself. However, WMU ached for its family of missionaries, international friends, and fellow members stretched around the world, who all suffered from the conflict. WMU certainly never claimed divine favor for America, but it *did* take a strong stand for patriotism, stressing the importance of preserving religious liberty. The Annie Armstrong Offering was frequently promoted in this decade with a theme of patriotism.

The War to End All Wars

World War II could not help but affect WMU. More and more women were pulled into the public workplace. Kathleen Mallory commented that war brought to the surface the value of having a smooth-running organization that could withstand the stress of missed meetings, restricted travel, and abbreviated publications.

The separation from Baptist sisters in other countries was traumatic. WMU continued their regular Lottie Moon Offering allocations for these lands and asked the

Foreign Mission Board to reserve these funds until the war was over. It was a wise and farsighted move, for it got postwar rehabilitation efforts off to a great start. Although WMU did not officially speak on the internment of Japanese Americans in the US, they immediately provided a Baptist ministry for those camps.

The war caused WMU enrollment to decline, but at the same time, contributions rose. WMU altered its schedules, travel, and programs as necessary. Even getting paper on which to print magazines was a challenge. At one point, Mallory asked two family friends in the US Congress to intercede so she could obtain paper to print *Royal Service.*

WMU's Annual Meeting in 1945 was cancelled because of travel restrictions. As America's population shifted towards military installations, WMUers helped establish new Woman's Missionary Society groups and start churches near the installations. And, as soon as Italy surrendered in 1943, WMU began sending food and clothes, and later established the same ministry to Japan.

War's Aftermath
About the time the war finally ended, Olive Martin became national president. It was a critical juncture, and Martin was a leader with skill, grace, and a sense of correctness that proved effective. WMU relief work went into high gear. Young women at the 1946 Young Woman's Auxiliary (YWA) camp gave a record $4,207 for relief. When the Annual Meeting took a relief offering, missionaries described the needs of their field, and Kathleen Mallory, greatly moved, knelt on the stage to pray. By 1947, WMU reported over $1 million dollars in relief funds—26 percent of the Southern Baptist Convention (SBC) total.

WMU initiated its own style of making peace through the Baptist World Alliance (BWA), as Olive Martin, along with WMU funds, brought Baptist women of Europe together to organize and pray. The fact that these countries had so recently been at war was not an issue at this highly strategic meeting of women with the same ultimate goal.

> Ayako Hino, later secretary of the BWA Women's Department, carried Japan's flag in the Roll Call of Nations at the 1950 Baptist World Congress in Cleveland, Ohio. Her body visibly shook with fear of carrying her country's flag in the US. WMU leaders were also apprehensive about audience reaction. But Christian unity prevailed when the BWA president, E. Oscar Johnson, called out to the audience, "We'll all rise for Japan."

Passing the Plate

The 1940s saw not only war but the end of the Depression and the end of board debt for Baptists. The WMU offerings continued, but national WMU began to relinquish control over how the offerings were spent. A general sum from the offerings began to go into the Foreign Mission Board (FMB) salary budget. Well into the 1940s, the Home Mission Board (HMB) was still supporting over half their missionaries with WMU money. At last, however, the Cooperative Program began providing the majority of the operating budget. Then both the HMB and WMU relaxed their rigidity about allocations.

Even after HMB debts were retired in 1944, however, HMB secretary J. B. Lawrence continued to acknowledge WMU's role in saving the Board. Near the end of the decade, when welcoming Alma Hunt as new WMU executive, Lawrence stated: "I don't know whether you realize the heritage of the organization you have come to serve or not, but I want you to know that there were years when the only home missionaries kept on the field were being kept by gifts through the Annie Armstrong offering. All the other funds that the HMB received from the denomination in those dark years had to go to pay off the debts of the HMB."[1]

Near the end of the decade, the FMB's Theron Rankin issued a challenge for foreign missions advance. In effect, what developed was two more-or-less equal streams of support: the Cooperative Program and WMU's offering. The Cooperative Program reflected the logic of Baptists; the offerings the heart. From 1946 on, WMU offerings outstripped the Cooperative Program in rate of growth.

The 1940s brought change for WMU employees in that Kathleen Mallory shifted her viewpoint somewhat on employee compensation and began setting up a wage scale. And, at the same time, WMU began to comply with wage and hour law regulations.

Woman's Missionary Union Training School and Producing Missionaries

At the beginning of the 1940s, the Woman's Missionary Union Training School in Louisville had outgrown it's size; and after recovering from a slump in enrollment during the Depression, it was time to build again. WMU invested nearly $300,000 to construct a beautiful building near the new seminary campus. True to form, the move was made without debt.

Traditionally, religious education was a female domain at the training school; however, by 1948 the seminary put pressure on the training school to grant a religious education degree to men. This specific degree actually qualified women for missionary appointment and church-related positions. As men were awarded a bachelor's degree in religious education from the training school, the denomination regarded the training school as another of the official seminaries. This was the beginning of the training school's evolvement into the Carver School of Missions and Social Work.

Training future missionaries became a higher priority after the war. Both mission boards were out of debt and able to support large numbers of personnel for the first time in 20 years. WMU decided to make "calling out the called" a focus for their membership. As thousands of girls attended WMU summer camps, a constant theme at the camps was considering God's call. A favorite *Royal Service* topic in 1946 was Why I Am a Missionary. And the 1946 Annual Meeting centered around the need for more missionaries.

Possibly because of the positive results of WMU's emphasis on the call of God, the FMB soon modified its appeal, stating that it also needed men. They encouraged WMU to "give of their sons to bear the message glorious," asking WMU to emphasize missionary careers in Royal Ambassadors (RA) as well as in YWA. WMU responded by giving the young men their own missions magazine, *Ambassador Life,* in 1946. They also sponsored Young Men's Missions Conferences during FMB week at Ridgecrest.

Missions Teaching and Campfire Building

Mission study remained popular throughout the war years. By 1946, WMU standards required every woman to read at least one missions book a year. The courses were so popular and the demand so great that national WMU had to stop awarding diplomas and seals. Instead, they encouraged Woman's Missionary Societies to hand out their own awards. By 1948, 513 churches reported that every Woman's Missionary Society member had read at least one missions book from the approved list. One reason for this kind of participation was a popular new reading program that WMU launched in 1945—the Missionary Round Table. National WMU compiled a list of study books, and women in the churches read the books and discussed them in missions groups.

Another effective educational tool that continued during this decade was camping. Most state WMUs had been sponsoring camps or house parties for GA, RA, and YWA members since the 1930s. By 1940, there were 25,000 campers, almost half of them in Texas, where camping really became a tradition. The camps rewarded participation in youngsters' WMU organizations and provided intensive times of training. Then camps spread to adults. By 1943, adult women in New Mexico were asking for a camp, and the popularity of missions camping and conferences resulted in Business Women's Circle meetings at Ridgecrest, North Carolina. This was the motivation for beginning WMU conferences at Ridgecrest.

Changes in a New Era

In February 1944, national president Laura Armstrong appointed a survey committee to plan for the postwar era, selecting her best friend, Cora McWilliams, former Missouri president, as chairman. The committee researched for a year, reporting to the WMU Executive Committee in January 1945. They knew without doubt that their recommendations would elicit heated discussion, for McWilliams found herself in opposition to both Armstrong and Mallory.

Actually, all of the committee's proposals eventually became reality, but the problem lay in the implication that almost everything about WMU needed major changes. The report was so controversial that Kathleen Mallory sealed it in the vault with orders that it not be seen without permission. Although it was phrased in polite tones, the report implied a loss of confidence in the officers and became yet another test of WMU's ability to handle diversity of opinion.

Among the controversial suggestions was the proposal that it was time for WMU to provide missions education for all church membership. The committee felt that WMU should have a closer relationship to the church program and that its program plans should involve WMU leaders in foreign lands as well. Further recommendations: WMU should have a closer relationship with each seminary's women's schools, and workers with youth and children should have greater status. Furthermore, WMU should confront the worsening racial crisis. Perhaps most controversial, the committee suggested that WMU should stop counting, reporting, and receiving credit for Cooperative Program contributions.

Although the report reflected many postwar values, they still seemed quite radical in 1945, and even revolutionary to many women. As soon as the meeting was over, Armstrong wrote to McWilliams, letting her know their friendship was intact. McWilliams replied just as graciously, saying she had never done anything so hard as to seem critical of Kathleen Mallory, whom "I love, admire and in whose judgment I have much confidence."[2]

The committee members expected their report to be buried, but not in the way that it was, by being placed in the vault. However, Mallory quietly implemented many of the proposals. Three years later, she ended her 36-year tenure. Alma Hunt came to the office without having to break the seal on the report envelope. She had innocently helped McWilliams with her clerical work 4 years earlier, never dreaming she would be the one to implement so many of the plans laid out in the report.

Postwar Growth Moves Beyond the South

Population shifts continued following World War II, and Baptist growth extended beyond the South. Prior agreements by Southern and Northern Baptists that defined where the two conventions would serve were no longer relevant. And, of course there was misunderstanding at first between the two conventions. Northern Baptists and

Southern Baptists worked through the situation and an amicable agreement was reached. In 1944, the SBC affirmed that its territory was unlimited. By the beginning of the next decade, Northern Baptists took the new name American Baptists. Typically, as new state conventions organized, WMUs were organized at the same time and became part of WMU, SBC. As the country grew, so did WMU. Hawaii WMU was formed in 1944 under the Foreign Mission Board's island ministries.[3]

Children's Work and Christmas in August

Children's organizations grew as well during this decade. In the late 1940s, WMU again asked the Brotherhood to discuss taking over some of the responsibility for the Royal Ambassadors organization. On a local level, many men were already RA leaders. The first man on the WMU staff, Ivyloy Bishop, came to national WMU in 1943 to do professional Royal Ambassadors work. During his 10 years, enrollment doubled. By 1949, more men than women were counselors for RA members.

The Sunbeam Band age span shrank during the 1940s. Preschoolers were separated from school-age children by 1942.

The beginning of the new decade marked the reintroduction of "box work" under a new name. Now called Christmas in August, WMU members packed boxes of supplies in August to send to home missionaries for Christmas distribution. At first adults participated in the project, but soon delegated it to children and youth. Children enthusiastically gathered and prepared thousands of dollars worth of items to send for home missions needs.

Trends in WMU Growth

In 1948, spurred by postwar trends, WMU leaders in most states saw a move toward evening meetings, even for women who worked at home. Families no longer had

Olive Burnette Brinson Martin: 1945–56

Olive Brinson was known as "Ollie" as a little girl growing up in Hampton, Virginia. Born in 1893, she didn't have early opportunities for higher education but was a brilliant student, handling a heavy academic load in high school. At age 19, Olive married George Martin. They lived in Norfolk, and she became local WMU president at the tender age of 22. Olive was known as WMU's ultimate strategist, a talent obvious from the start. She was involved in dozens of projects and activities in her church and association, and this vast experience later aided her when she became national president. Olive Martin was chosen Virginia state president in 1925.

Under unusual circumstances due to the death of Laura Armstrong, Martin became president of national WMU in 1945. The next year she was elected to a full term. Her terms of service were marked by creative progress and unprecedented growth. There were many changes during her years, and she handled them with graciousness and correctness.

Olive was ahead of the times in racial progress, dealing ably with sensitive social and political issues. And on a worldwide scale, her organizational talents made real inroads. Because of her passion and skills, Baptist Women's Day of Prayer was born.

After retiring from the national presidency, Olive Martin was an active local WMU member, and continued to aid the Baptist Women's Department of the BWA, of which she was architect and builder. Olive Martin died in 1972, at age 78. That molder of magnificent organizations left an enduring impact upon the missions thrust of America's Woman's Missionary Union, and on Baptist women around the world.

From *Laborers Together with God* by Catherine Allen (WMU, 1987).

servants, live-in relatives, and older siblings at home. The American lifestyle was changing and WMU would change as well, with meetings scheduled at a variety of times and with nurseries provided. By 1950, WMU membership surpassed the 1 million mark.

Evangelism and Community Missions

As usual, WMU cooperated with the SBC in combined efforts to evangelize the nation. The SBC proposed to win a million converts in observance of the 1945 Convention centennial. Woman enthusiastically joined in the drive, especially emphasizing cottage prayer meetings. A report from the Texas evangelism secretary gives an idea of the impact WMU had. Women comprised 90 percent of the attendance at morning revival meetings, 95 percent at prayer meetings, 95 percent of the personal evangelism workers, and 75 percent of evening service attenders. The annual baptism count was 256,600 (an increase of 39,879 from the previous year). Kathleen Mallory said, "It is humbly believed that quite a few of the baptisms were in part at least [a] . . . result of community missions."[4]

To invigorate personal service, WMU renamed the effort Community Missions in 1942, emphasizing the importance of soul-winning. Mary Christian, a former professor at the training school, became a national staff member with WMU. She managed community missions, giving primary attention to the race issue and to evangelism. Then in 1949, community missions became a full-time staff position, headed by Edith Stokely, a former campus minister. In step with trends of the times, community missions concentrated on spiritual and moral needs.

New Leadership

The all-time tenure record for any Southern Baptist chief executive was Kathleen Mallory's 36 years. Woman's Missionary Union really entered a new era in 1948, when Alma Hunt succeeded Mallory.[5] In her acceptance speech, Hunt promised WMU two things: commitment to the people of WMU and commitment to its purposes. She never wavered in fulfilling both promises. And in her first annual report in 1949, Hunt asserted, "Yea I have a goodly heritage. . . .We must build on the foundation which has been laid. We must underscore with our heart's blood the eternal unfaded verities, and in addition make our own contribution."[6]

And build and contribute they did, this new generation of women. Hunt's election as executive secretary marked the beginning of the greatest growth in WMU history, and arguably, the period of most change as well. Running through every change, every innovation, however, was the silver strand that had bound the women of WMU together since the very beginning: an unwavering focus on giving the gospel to the world.

9
1951–1960

For the first time in almost 40 years, WMU did not enter a decade with Kathleen Mallory as executive secretary. The second half of the century was ushered in with Alma Hunt signaling a new era in women's missions advance. President Olive Martin bridged the tenures of both executive secretaries and served with Hunt until 1956. Marie Mathis of Texas was elected national president that year, and she and Alma Hunt became a formidable duo in leading and inspiring missions advance.

Change was certainly in the air for the South and the nation as a whole during the 1950s. One of the biggest changes centered around civil rights. The racial controversy became so heated that many southerners were too inflamed to tolerate the mention of Black ministry. Executive secretary Alma Hunt felt her job was to "keep the cars from being uncoupled from the train." Race was often mentioned in WMU magazines, and each mention brought a barrage of hate mail and cancellations.

Even if leaders would have liked to have swept the issue aside until a cooler time, they could not. Foreign missionaries and Baker James Cauthen of the Foreign Mission Board (FMB) constantly reminded WMU that news of racial violence in Southern Baptist territory was destroying missions efforts abroad. Here, as in other issues, the international perspective brought social awareness at home. WMU took a progressive stand through its speakers at every Annual Meeting for two decades.

An effort to integrate the Young Woman's Auxiliary (YWA) Conference was tabled in 1954, but gained approval in 1958, provided African Americans were a legitimate part of WMU's organized work. WMU integrated its Louisville training school in 1952, at the same time admitting males.

Woman's Missionary Union Training School and the Carver School of Missions and Social Work

In what would become a decade devoted to education, WMU's training school reached a crossroads. Not knowing where to turn next, the women consulted their longtime mentor, W. O. Carver. As a student, Carver had been an eyewitness to the 1888 founding of WMU. Stemming from a deep respect for women, beginning with his mother and extending through analysis of Scripture, he believed Christianity placed responsibility and opportunity equally upon women and men.

Carver established the first formal department of missions and comparative religions in higher education at Southern Seminary in 1899. He became Woman's Missionary Union Training School's first professor and lectured almost every Woman's Missionary Union Training School student until his death in 1954. The Southern Baptist man most knowledgeable about missions was also the one who did the most to lift and encourage women.

When, in 1952, Southern Seminary offered to make the Woman's Missionary Union Training School its religious education school for men and women, WMU sought advice from Carver to determine how to answer. Although retired from the seminary, Carver was still on the male advisory board of the Woman's Missionary Union Training School.

Carver gave his advice, and Woman's Missionary Union Training School followed it. WMU decided to magnify the school's original specialties of missions and social work. They voted to drop the antiquated name "training school" and to admit students regardless of sex or race. In cooperation, the seminary announced it would open a school of religious education in the fall of 1953 and open its doors to women.

As usual, once he had helped the women catch a vision, Carver went home to let them work out details in their own way. Unanimously, they renamed the school the Carver School of Missions and Social Work.

The Carver School launched new studies, including literacy missions and seminars in missionary problems. Courses were added in phonetics, linguistics, cultural anthropology, world revolution, child welfare, law, social pathology, and social casework. The first African American student was enrolled in 1952; the first male graduated in 1955; and the first master of science in missions was awarded in 1955.

All of these advances mandated more money. In 1952 WMU asked the Southern Baptist Convention (SBC) Executive Committee for an additional one-half percent of the Cooperative Program to add to the school's funding. The request was denied because the school was not controlled by the SBC—a point that had never been raised before. The pressure for Cooperative Program funds triggered committee appointment to study the needs for theological education. A compromise solution was found. The Carver School would be transferred in 1956 to SBC ownership, but trustees would be named by WMU.

It was not altogether a successful arrangement. By 1957 a management consultant study found decreased enrollment due to perceptions that the school was for women. Women's schools were in national decline. Women who wanted theological training could get it at any of six Southern Baptist seminaries. The missions education focus was too narrow and in advance of its time to obtain accreditation. When itemized, the problems were numerous. By 1961 the trustees negotiated a merger of the school into Southern Seminary, which later created the Carver School of Church Social Work.

Stewardship

The creditors were no longer at the mission boards' doors in the 1950s, so WMU stepped back for a more general study of stewardship. A series of stewardship study books for all ages was issued in 1954, and state stewardship chairmen were invited to Birmingham for a meeting in May 1956. Hunt explained that the emphasis on giving one-tenth for the church would not be lessened, but that the nine-tenths remaining must also be used in a Christian way. Moreover, WMU became concerned about Christian distinctives in acquisition of money. Stewardship conferences rippled across the country. In 1955 the WMU Executive Board adopted a stewardship policy for education of children. The time-honored phrase *Tithes and Offerings* was replaced in the 1955–56 Plan of Work with the broader term *Stewardship of Possessions,* emphasizing WMU's belief that stewardship was "a principle to be instilled, rather than a method to be installed."

During this decade, Annie Armstrong's interest in western missions was reflected in the use of her namesake offering in the 1950s and 1960s, as the Annie Armstrong Offering allocations were used to focus on the West and pioneer work.

Birthday Candles and Prayers

The missionary calendar, first included in *Royal Service* in 1918, had grown so large that WMU needed to devise a system to avoid overlooking someone. The solution? In 1952 the calendar of prayer began to list each missionary on his or her birthday. Field of service and type of work were also noted. This became a popular approach and better connected readers with missionaries. Missionaries began receiving hundreds of birthday cards and miraculous support.

The weeks of prayer were also renovated in the 1950s. First introduced in 1895, the weeks of prayer became churchwide in 1956. All Southern Baptists observed the weeks of prayer in regular worship services, and often churchwide banquets, dramas, early morning breakfast groups, and other events were held in combination with the emphases. Special literature encouraged eight days of prayer at home. WMU remained committed to the idea that the special missions offerings were not to be promoted aside from prayer.

The 1950s were indeed golden years of prayer. President Marie Mathis prompted the development of WMU's spiritual emphasis. Along with literature and promotion, WMU prayer retreats were an effective way to involve women in missions. Prayer was later credited for bringing WMU to its peak enrollment during that era.

Teach Me to Read

WMU's literacy emphases had waned in previous decades, but were revived in 1946. Frank C. Laubach, who was to popularize literacy missions with his World Literacy Crusade, spoke that year at the WMU Annual Meeting. His wife spoke at the 1950 Annual Meeting. Their presentations sparked a new interest in teaching others to read.

In the early 1950s Laubach and his staff visited the Carver School of Missions and Social Work to train students in literacy techniques. Baylor University then established a literacy center, teaching WMU groups how to teach reading. These techniques were used not only for people totally unable to read, but also for persons learning English as a second language.

As WMU organizations for children and youth rapidly grew in the 1950s, community missions was part of their curriculum. For the youngest, community missions was simplified as Helping Others for Jesus' Sake. As they studied books about community missions, they were inspired to participate. Girls and teens who wanted to progress through the ranks of their organizations (Forward Steps) were required be personally engaged in community missions projects. As expected in children's activities, efforts were as much about education for the doers as about social change for the recipients. By 1961, the last year WMU reported community missions statistics, 63 percent of WMU organizations reported involvement.

Internationals and Language Ministries

In the 1950s WMU recognized a unique ministry opportunity. They began to take note of temporary residents from abroad—internationals. Many state WMUs helped host conferences and house parties for international students at Thanksgiving and Christmas. Many states worked with colleges to place internationals in WMU members' homes for holidays. But more than friendship needed to be extended. In 1954 the Executive Board of WMU invited the officers of the Hispanic WMU organizations to attend its meetings. These meetings helped keep the top Hispanic WMU leaders informed of organizational methods.

Mission Study and Publications

After World War II, mission study helped women adjust to a dangerous and shrinking world they had underestimated before. They studied missions to understand the daily newspaper headlines. They studied out of concern for world revolution, war, nationalism, and racism. Mission study grew to gigantic proportions in this era.

Mission study might have been encouraged by a general trend of women enrolling in adult education classes. Undoubtedly, WMU's emphasis on prayer also fueled the education fire. As women focused on prayer for missionaries and their work, they were compelled to study about the missions field. Martha McIntosh, that very first national president, called prayer the flame, missions information the fuel. After 1957, circle meetings included mission study. Each circle pursued a balanced diet of study, prayer, giving, and local missions.

Mission study was the focus of new magazines for children in 1953. *Sunbeam Activities,* a quarterly magazine for Sunbeam leaders, was introduced, along with *Tell,* a missions magazine for girls, which replaced *World Comrades.* The initial subscription list exceeded 70,000, and in its second year reached 94,000, boasting WMU's second largest circulation.

Although Spanish literature had been supported by WMU funds for decades, it was in 1955 that the first US-based WMU magazine was published in Spanish. A condensed translation of *Royal Service* was published under the name *Nuestra Tarea.*

As of October 1, 1957, WMU transferred literature, magazine subscription lists, and 127,656 Royal Ambassadors (RA) boys to the Brotherhood Commission. Certainly, this has been perceived as the most traumatic action in the history of WMU before its 1970 reorganization. The financial impact was significant, and some women doubted the Brotherhood Commission would live up to its promises to keep missions in the organization's forefront. However, the organization bloomed under Brotherhood's leadership. RA enrollment more than doubled in 7 years—a faster growth rate than under WMU.

Cardboard Boxes and Mail

By the late 1940s, WMU had again outgrown its office space at the Comer Building. When Hunt took office, she was confronted by the cramped, hot rooms and sacks of unopened magazine orders in corridors. Along with the stacks of magazines to be mailed was an order from the fire marshal to clear the corridors or go to jail.

At the January 1949 meeting of the Executive Committee, when local members were decorating for the luncheon, they decided to feature a model of their ideal WMU headquarters building. With no definite blueprints, they built a replica of a handsome new building recently completed in Birmingham. It was an insurance company's office with limestone columns, brass doors, and an elegant lobby on one of Birmingham's main streets.

As the committee struggled with an architect to design an economical building as beautiful as the luncheon centerpiece, they grew discouraged. However, 2 years later their dream became a reality. In January 1951, the very building the women had admired became their own. At a cost of $500,000, less a $25,000 gift by the owner, WMU acquired the building at 600 North 20th Street, a short walking distance from the Comer building. It was paid for in an unprecedented 2 years. Even before Hunt signed the purchase contract, the Executive Committee had convened in the building's auditorium to sing "Praise God, from Whom All Blessings Flow." The completed building housed not only a growing staff, but also a growing collection of important artwork and curios bestowed by friends and missionaries from around the world.

SBC Expansion Years

In 1953, WMU of the Northwest Baptist Convention began affiliates in Canada. Colorado WMU was organized in November 1955. And, expansion was not limited to the West. In 1957, Paul S. and Ava Leach James left a pastorate of 3,000 members in Atlanta and exchanged their five-bedroom, three-bath house for three rooms in a New York City high-rise. James became pastor of a small congregation, Manhattan Baptist Church, and Ava began organizing women's groups in the area, stretching as far as 350 miles away. By 1960 the resulting churches formed the Northeast Baptist Association and Northeast Baptist WMU.

When Ava pleaded for help with her efforts, volunteers brought training teams from Ohio and Maryland, but more were needed. Alma Hunt conferred with the Home Mission Board (HMB), and they agreed to provide funds for a full-time WMU staff member to travel to pioneer areas. She would have her home base in Birmingham under WMU management, but would be jointly employed by HMB and WMU. Bernice Elliott, the experienced secretary for WMU young people's work in Arizona, was hired as the WMU staff member for pioneer work.

Elliott was one of many professionals added to the WMU staff during the 1950s. The population explosion that made WMU membership mushroom was quickly felt in the national WMU office. A panel of age-level experts was hired in 1955, and a management consultant was retained in 1956 to advise in reorganizing the staff of 90.

More years of advance lay ahead, as well as unforeseen events which would lead to fresh challenges and innovative approaches. The underlying goal of sharing the gospel, however, never faltered.

Marie Wiley Mathis: 1956–63, 1969–75

National WMU had a penchant for charismatic and unique leaders, and Marie Mathis was certainly no exception. Born in Texas in 1903, little Marie Wiley was a beautiful baby, and that beauty of features was reflected throughout her life in the beauty of her manifest faith and commitment. Marie married a banker, Robert Lee Mathis, and their only child, Jane, was born in 1928. Marie became active in the local Woman's Missionary Society. She was also an acknowledged young socialite in Texas; but when confronted with the various interests and needs pulling her in several directions, she opted for devotion to missions. This choice was to lead her from local to worldwide arenas.

When the Mathis family moved to Dallas, Marie became indispensable to state WMU leadership as she volunteered to meet one need after another, excelling in all she did. She became youth secretary for Texas Baptists and blazed new trails of excellence with youth, eventually coming to the attention of national WMU.

Marie Mathis was a woman of boundless energy and diverse talents. When her husband died suddenly in 1946, the widowed Marie accepted a position on the staff of First Baptist Church; and then in 1947 she became president of Texas WMU. She also accepted a position as social director at Baylor University, initiating all sorts of innovative student activities. Her skills, from presenting dramas, to decorating, to planning pageants, became legendary.

When Marie, as state president, began promoting the Lottie Moon offering for all church members, it revolutionized missions giving in Texas. Within a year she led Texas Baptists to give more than one-third of the total national offering. Soon she had a seat on the Foreign Mission Board, and not long afterwards, she also served on the Southern Baptist Convention Executive Committee.

In 1956, Marie Mathis was elected WMU national president. Marie, a very devout woman, was noted for stopping any proceedings for a time of prayer. Among the numerous distinctions of her years in office was her endorsement of churchwide promotion of the special offerings. This churchwide plan made a vast difference in funds received.

The world became the venue of Marie Mathis, and she became a leading advocate for women worldwide. During her presidency from 1956 to 1963, Marie Mathis was noted for working hard and then keeping quiet until her statement of opinion would make a difference. Among her stellar talents was her ability to sense what a group wanted to do and then help them do it.

Marie Mathis agreed to return to the position of national president in 1969 and aid in leading WMU through a time when women's roles were rapidly changing in society. Her committed and steady leadership lent much-needed stability during a period of rapid change.

In 1970, she became president of the Women's Department of the Baptist World Alliance. In those years the indomitable Marie Mathis was showered with awards for outstanding leadership and remained stalwart in guiding WMU through repeated periods of change. Her final challenge as president was to smooth the transition of Alma Hunt's leadership to Carolyn Weatherford as executive head.

Marie Mathis never admitted to illness and appeared to ignore the cancer that was seeping the life out of her. She died in 1985, mourned and honored across the nation as well as abroad. The life and ministry of Marie Mathis has been imprinted indelibly in the history of Woman's Missionary Union.

From *Laborers Together with God* by Catherine Allen (WMU, 1987).

Alma Hunt: 1948–74

A legend in her own time. That is Alma Hunt. "You have a habit of lingering in the hearts of those who have known you," a leading WMU figure said of the young Alma Hunt more than a half-century ago. And she has continued lingering in the hearts of thousands of Baptists worldwide, into a new century and a new millennium. For 26 years she served as WMU executive secretary, invigorating and inspiring not only the entire organization but all of the SBC as well.

Born in Roanoke, Virginia, in 1909, Alma Fay Hunt grew up in First Baptist Church where her father was a deacon, and her mother was a pillar of Woman's Missionary Society (WMS). As a little girl, she often heard her grandmother comment, "Alma Hunt will talk herself to death." And talk she did, winning a place in the hearts of an entire denomination. Growing up in Sunbeam Band and GA, Alma early opened her heart to the world.

She became a schoolteacher during the Depression, although still just a teenager herself; and during the summers she was administrator of YWCA camps. But more than any other organizational influence in her life was Young Woman's Auxiliary (YWA). Her pastor's wife led YWA, and Alma quickly became a leader herself, inspiring all who came in contact with her. She switched to directing recreation at GA and YWA camps at Ridgecrest, North Carolina, during the summers, then having opportunity to observe and learn from national WMU leaders like Ethlene Cox, Juliette Mather, and Kathleen Mallory.

In 1944, Alma Hunt became dean of women at William Jewell College in Liberty, Missouri, and spent her summers at Columbia University, earning a master's degree in student personnel administration. During her years at William Jewell, national WMU leaders observed this promising young leader as she developed her singular leadership skills. When approached by WMU for the position of executive secretary, Alma doubted her qualifications. Although she had administrative skills, she thought that she was not a speaker. Ironically, she evolved into one of the outstanding speakers of her time.

Finally convinced, Alma accepted the position in 1948 and never looked back. She focused her exceptional gifts and energy on leading WMU. During her administration, WMU experienced its most successful growth. It was also a period of monumental national change, but she led tirelessly, bringing WMU into the last half of the twentieth century to be clearly on the cutting edge of missions advance.

Possibly Alma Hunt's most remarkable contribution to the character of WMU was to lead it to closer harmony with the Southern Baptist Convention and its churches. She became president of the SBC Inter-Agency Council in 1955 and demonstrated an uncanny ability to work with other executives. And the most massive overhaul of WMU age-level organizations and publications occurred during her administration. Alma demonstrated her unique leadership talents as she held WMU to its purposes even as it maintained organizational effectiveness.

Alma Hunt was a world traveler on mission with God and left the impact of her vision on countless lives. Extremely active in Baptist World Alliance (BWA), she influenced thousands, and in 1970 was elected a vice-president of the world Baptist body.

She stepped aside on her 65th birthday. However, retirement was a misnomer for Alma Hunt. For 10 years, she worked with the Foreign Mission Board as consultant for women's work overseas, traveling to more than 100 countries. And through the years she kept in touch with hundreds of her "far-flung friends."

Alma Hunt celebrated her 96th birthday in 2005. She continues to "linger in the hearts of those who have known her," and in the hearts of the multiple thousands who have been blessed by her ministry.

From *Laborers Together with God* by Catherine Allen (WMU, 1987) and *Courage and Hope: The Stories of Ten Baptist Women Ministers*, edited by Pamela R. Durso and Keith E. Durso (Mercer University Press, 2005).

10
1961–1970

The decade of the 1960s in the South is noted for the crisis of southern racial relations. This social dilemma profoundly impacted all Southern Baptists. Pressures became so intense that women and men curtailed long-standing projects out of fear for themselves and for those participating in the projects. In Woman's Missionary Union, Helen Fling followed Marie Mathis as national president in 1963, and then Mathis again in 1969 accepted the job. These two strong leaders, in tandem with Alma Hunt, guided WMU during this precarious period.

Quietly, WMU leaders continued their long-standing relationship with African American women. They put money, property, and encouragement in the hands of African American women so that they might continue needed projects. Radically, WMU publications encouraged the women's efforts through its magazines, giving more attention to race than any other Southern Baptist publication. A 1964 statement in the Young Woman's Auxiliary (YWA) magazine, *The Window of YWA*, which especially elicited cancellations and criticism, urged Southern Baptist young people to "involve themselves positively—under God's leadership" in the racial revolution. T. B. Maston, in a survey of Baptist literature, noted, "Woman's Missionary Union has generally made and continues to make the most directly challenging approach to the whole area of race."[1]

The WMU national office was both physically and figuratively in the middle of the visual civil rights conflict. Located on Sixth Avenue North, in downtown Birmingham, the headquarters building was only blocks away from the city hall and courthouse where many protests occurred. National WMU leaders found themselves criticized by both—considered troublemakers by some southerners and cowards by northerners.

In an era when most southern African Americans and Anglos had ceased communication, Baptist women leaders found a way to maintain their contact through the North American Baptist Women's Union (NABWU) of the Baptist World Alliance Women's Department. In 1962 NABWU elected two officers who scarcely knew each other, even though they both lived in Birmingham. For president they elected Mildred McMurry, who was Anglo, and for secretary they elected Margery B. Gaillard, who was African American. Quickly forming a bond and joining forces, these two women returned to Birmingham and quietly established an interracial group that prayed their way through the crisis.

Situations had already changed elsewhere in the Southern Baptist Convention (SBC). WMU members in the South became aware that Southern Baptist churches in the West and North had African American members and that those African Americans were solid, contributing WMU members. Helen Fling, who followed Mathis as president, moved to New York and an integrated church. There she saw firsthand the contributions that African American women could make to the missions effort. African Americans as Southern Baptists were a minority, but they were welcomed and visible in WMU by 1965.

Pray and Study and Study to Pray

The emphasis on prayer begun in 1955 continued into this decade, both personally and corporately. Missions prayer groups were instituted in 1968, and short-term prayer projects followed. WMU provided prayer support for the Crusade of the Americas, a simultaneous evangelistic crusade in North, South, and Central America in 1968 and 1969. At the suggestion of Marie Mathis, the WMU prayer plan was called PACT: Praying for the Americas Crusade Together.

This crusade was WMU's first venture into printing literature in languages other than Spanish. Prayer registration cards and guidance folders were printed in Spanish, Portuguese, and English. More than 1 million pieces were distributed, resulting in more than 50,000 persons or groups from 49 states and 27 countries requesting to be matched with prayer partners.

WMU members prayed specifically, after studying mission situations. Enrollment in mission study classes and the use of books as the basis of study remained a phenomenal success. In 1961 more than 590,000 people read missions books, and almost 125,000 book study classes were held.

By this time, the understanding of what constituted mission study and missions education had shifted. WMU increasingly emphasized a week-by-week study in organizational meetings. WMU magazines, now with a circulation of almost 1 million, provided an educationally sound, balanced approach to missions knowledge. By 1965 leaders were stating that mission study meant not just teaching a book, but long-range participation in organized study.

WMU slowly moved into being its own book publisher. In addition to the 1950s methods manuals, in this decade WMU published books on missions philosophy. Books in the "Aims" series focused on enlistment, soul-winning, stewardship, world awareness, and spiritual life development and were enormously popular.

In 1966 WMU joined with the Sunday School Board and Brotherhood Commission to coordinate Sunday School curriculum that reinforced missions topics taught by WMU and Brotherhood. The attempt proved too cumbersome, and WMU dropped out after three years. The Sunday School continued using the series under the name Life and Work Curriculum.

WMU has always had a special love for the children of missionaries—MKs (missionary kids). Dating back to 1918, when women spontaneously gave $1,629 for the education of four children whose mother had died as a missionary in Africa, MK education became an important undertaking for WMU.

The Margaret Home, where MKs were housed there while studying in America during the early 1900s, was eventually sold and its proceeds became the start of a fund for MKs' education. The income from the invested money helped MKs attend a school of their choice, something the mission boards could not afford to do. The fund was made a memorial to Kate Chambers's missions-minded mother, and became known as the Margaret Fund. By 1961 so many students were receiving assistance that WMU turned administration of the program to the respective boards.

Revolutionary Changes

Turbulence seemed to rule American life in the 1960s. Southern Baptists were troubled about growing social problems: crime rates that soared to nine times the rate of the 1950s, campus war protests, race riots, and youth interest in recreational drugs. Prayer in public schools was ruled unconstitutional in 1962, and Eastern religions became popular. By the end of the decade, the moral pendulum had taken a full swing to the left.

The changes also caught the attention of WMU. When Helen Fling became WMU president in 1963, she asked the WMU staff to draft a WMU plan for the age of revolution. She reactivated Christian social ministry as a means of personal missions work, being convinced that study was worthless unless it resulted in action. The resulting program was called mission action. WMU defined mission action as "organized effort of a church to minister and to witness to persons of special need or circumstance who are not immediate prospects for the church."

As American society grew more troubled and revolutionary, mission action made more sense to Baptists. Although in the past WMU had not officially involved itself in social causes, women changed their minds during this decade. In 1968 the WMU program recognized that women might address target issues as well as target groups. Among the issues considered were family problems, gambling, pornography, obscenity, substance abuse, racial tensions, and economic problems. WMU wrote manuals outlining those problems, encouraging women to confront them.

Churches were encouraged to start mission action efforts with a community survey. The 1967 Annual Meeting focused on the need for Christian social work. WMU teamed with the Home Mission Board (HMB) and Brotherhood Commission to publish a *Mission Action Survey Guide*, along with guidebooks for work with internationals, the sick, juvenile rehabilitation, language groups, and economically disadvantaged. In less than six months more than 60,000 copies of the guides had been sold. Later, other target groups included prisoners, military personnel, alcoholics, drug abusers, migrants, travelers and tourists, nonreaders, aging, unwed parents, the institutionalized, and minority groups.

Volunteer Missions Trips

WMU women had donated time for missions projects since the last century. However, the 1960s formalized some of these efforts. In 1962 WMU Executive Board member Susie Illingworth, a widow with grown children, heard Wendell Belew of the HMB speak about pioneer missions during the Week of Prayer for Home Missions. After the service she told Belew she wished she could help in pioneer work.

Three weeks later Belew called, outlining the need of Nicy Murphy in Colorado for help with summer WMU camps and leader training. Illingworth paid her own expenses to spend the summer in Colorado, North and South Dakota, Montana, and Wyoming.

This experience prompted the WMU Executive Board to ask the Home Mission Board to work out a women's volunteer plan, and thus creating the Christian Service Corps in 1965. Volunteer missions trips became a popular focus for many women and families.

All Southern Baptists Are Not Southern

The decade of the 1960s was a time of expansion for WMU, within the church and within the nation. As WMU began focusing on teaching missions to the whole church, they also began focusing on states outside the South. While supporting the SBC Thirty Thousand Movement, a campaign to establish 30,000 new congregations by the 150th anniversary of the first Southern Baptist Convention, women struck out to spread missions education to new congregations and in every preaching point. WMU magazines and other publications featured pioneer areas and new state expansions. By 1964 almost 25,000 new congregations had been started, resulting in 6,682 new churches.

Language missions work and resulting ethnic WMU organizations grew during this decade. Work was growing in many states including Texas, New Mexico, and Puerto Rico. Internationals living in northern states were asking for meeting instructions in their own languages. In 1969 Alma Hunt worked with the HMB staff to arrange the first conference for Spanish-speaking women at Glorieta Baptist Conference Center (now LifeWay Conference Center at Glorieta) in New Mexico. Ethnic leadership training courses soon became a standard item for WMU conferences. In 1961, Bernice Elliott, promotion associate in pioneer areas, began traveling to the new SBC areas as a joint HMB/WMU staff member. On one West Coast trip she spoke in 38 different language churches.

Unity in Church Work

SBC organizations, including WMU, developed a plan to become more unified in their approach to church work during this decade. Each organization agreed to state their purposes as "tasks." For WMU, the philosophy of tasks within the church was a shift in how they perceived themselves. In the past WMU had carried out its purposes among those signed up as members. Now, since these tasks were to be churchwide, WMU was accepting responsibility for every church participant, just like the Sunday School Board or some other SBC agency. It would be leading the entire church in missions, not just women and children.

WMU kept pace with the changes going on within the SBC, but they were determined to stick to their missions purpose. They established these organizational tasks in 1964:
- Teach missions.
- Lead persons to participate in missions.
- Provide organization and leadership for special missions projects of the church.
- Provide and interpret information regarding the work of the church and the denomination.

WMU's New Look

In retrospect, changes in the nation and in the SBC were so radical that WMU could have been destroyed between 1968 and 1971. However, WMU was built on a firm foundation. The tenacity and vision of leaders and members who were fully committed to being "laborers together" ensured that the organization stood firm and remained dedicated to its purpose of missions education.

Prompted by national unrest, women's changing roles, and the Southern Baptist agency changes, WMU restated its program and redesigned its organizations between 1964 and 1970. The Sunday School Board, WMU, and Brotherhood agreed to establish programs and products so that churches might develop a united, coordinated program in 1970. All agencies would have four basic age groupings. That meant WMU had to restructure its organizations and add new periodicals.

Although it took a lot of planning, WMU hoped that the dramatic age-level changes that were unveiled in October 1970 would combat the enrollment decline of 1965. But, on the contrary, after the changes were made, WMU continued to lose members, although at a slower rate, for four years. Then figures increased slightly and stabilized. Yet with all the changes taking place, one thing remained constant—contributions to missions.

The new age level for women aged 30 and up was named Baptist Women. WMU also added a quarterly periodical for WMU general officers and church administration, *Dimension*. The popular study methods and Round Table Book Club remained unchanged.

Young adult women aged 18 through 29 received their own organization, Baptist Young Women (BYW), and their own magazine, *Contempo*.[2]

The girls organization also received an overhaul. Girls' Auxiliary was renamed Girls in Action. This represented the spirit of the organization and preserved the popular GA initials. The girls' individual achievement plan was called Missions Adventures and featured six levels of activity. The leaders received a new periodical, *Aware*, and the girls' magazine was *Discovery*.

Acteens®, the organization for girls in grades 7 through 12, was launched at the beginning of this new decade—1970. Their individual achievement plan, StudiAct, involved teenage girls in mission study and action through missions projects. They were recognized in five levels of advance: Queen, Queen with Scepter, Queen Regent, Queen Regent in Service and Service Aide.

A new age level for preschool boys and girls was launched at this time also. They were called Mission Friends®, and became the successor of Sunbeams. The magazine, *Start,* gave instructions for Mission Friends classes. WMU stressed that even infants could gain foundations in missions if cared for in a proper environment.

WMU leadership was unhappy to lose six-, seven- and eight-year-old boys, who in the grouping-grading reorganization became Royal Ambassadors (RA) members.

WMU and Giving

Throughout its history, Woman's Missionary Union had been leaders in giving among Baptists. This did not change in the decade of the 1960s. Foreign Mission Board (FMB) secretary Baker J. Cauthen told his Board that the Lottie Moon Offering ought to be considered as regular dependable income. He did not see that as changing. Cauthen described the Cooperative Program and the Lottie Moon Offering as twin tracks on which the train of foreign missions was equally propelled. By 1961, the Lottie Moon Offering surpassed the Cooperative Program to become the largest single source of foreign missions funds. Additionally, in 1961, the Annie Armstrong Offering for the first time provided more than 40 percent of HMB income. And in a short time, it also outstripped the Cooperative Program as the HMB's largest single source of income.

Helen Long Fling: 1963–69

Born in Texas in 1914 to a frontier Baptist pastor, Helen Long grew up to challenge new frontiers of leadership in mission service and commitment. A lovely blonde with a captivating smile and a brilliant mind, Helen was uniquely prepared by God for leadership in long years to come. Her only ambition was to be the wife of a good Baptist layman. She even became engaged to one. Then a young evangelist, Robert Fling, preached a revival in her church, and the rest is history. In short order Helen broke her engagement to one and was soon engaged to the other. She became Mrs. Robert Fling in 1934. It was an unusual honeymoon for a 19-year-old Texas girl—cruising to Europe to attend the BWA Congress in Berlin. The Congress, especially the women's meetings, opened up a whole new world to the girl from Texas, and it was a revelation. The newlyweds committed themselves to service wherever God wanted to use them.

The determined Helen Fling graduated from college after the birth of their daughter, Sheila. Later the Flings adopted their infant son, Mike.

Nurtured by older WMU women, Helen was being groomed for leadership. But, even when selected as associational president, she did not feel capable. Such feelings, however, throughout her years of service never diminished the impact of the achievements she left in her wake. Missions began at home for the Flings, in their sacrificial giving as well as their time.

From one level of leadership to another, WMU recognized Helen's potential. In 1957 she became recording secretary for WMU, SBC, and her role as speaker and writer continued to expand. In 1962 she wrote the popular WMU book *Enlistment for Missions*. She was elected president of national WMU in May 1963, making the vow: "I promise you the best that I can become." She ended up presiding over a tumultuous period in WMU history, from the racial issue with its many challenges, to the upheavals caused by the Southern Baptist church programming movement. Helen displayed a growing spirituality in the face of each challenge, lending a calmness and a steady hand to provide stability to an ever-evolving situation. It was Helen Fling who led in drafting the concepts and literature for mission action.

Through all her years as president, she served on the Southern Baptist Convention Executive Committee. While still national president, Helen became a literal part of home missions as she and Bob moved to New York, where he became pastor-director for the county and the first full-time pastor of a tiny Westchester County church. After one year, Helen resigned her presidency in order to devote full time to home missions. Not surprisingly, she was a sparkplug for WMU in New York State, calling for help from WMU friends across the nation. She continued to represent WMU and to write as well.

Then the Flings moved further afield, going at the request of the Foreign Mission Board to Germany to pastor for a year. Then followed five years of promotion and travel for the Home Mission Board. Bob Fling died in 1982, and in 1985, Helen retired in Birmingham and continued speaking and promoting WMU. Daily prayer for a huge number of missionaries who were personal friends became a hallmark of Helen's days, and she reached around the world through their manifold ministries. Helen Fling's unequivocal personal commitment to missions has touched thousands of lives on every continent and continues to make a difference—even into the new millennium.

From *Laborers Together with God* by Catherine Allen (WMU, 1987)

Changing Times

The social changes that the 1960s brought to the nation had their effect on WMU as well. Until the mid-1960s half of WMU's members were adults. After that, children became the majority members. Why? The women's liberation movement gave women more choices of what to do with their lives. WMU found itself competing with careers, classes, and general social chaos. Until the mid-1960s, WMU statistics had declined only during the world wars and the Great Depression.

As the nation changed, so did WMU. The organization continued to adapt to meet women's needs. In 1968 Woman's Missionary Society (WMS) focused on teaching women in small groups instead of the traditional circles. A group might choose to concentrate on current missions, missions Bible study, mission action, prayer, or other options. A woman could belong to several groups. Before, WMS leaders had assigned women to circles. Now the members made their own choices. And, some chose to drop out, confused by so many choices. Although the number of organizations remained steady, almost 100,000 members were lost in three years. More changes were ahead.

11
1971–1980

Society was changing and so was WMU and the Southern Baptist Convention (SBC). The dynamic duo of Marie Mathis and Alma Hunt stood firm when confronted by media regarding monumental social changes. And, Carolyn Weatherford, who became WMU executive director in 1974 following Hunt's retirement, along with Christine Gregory, who followed Mathis as president in 1975, formed a competent and diplomatic team offering a spirit of goodwill and unity when confronted with multiple changes in the SBC.

Woman's Changing Roles
Southern Baptists in general and WMU in particular chose to ignore the women's liberation movement. WMU publications took no note of it until 1970. The possibility of changed roles for women in church was scarcely mentioned before that year.

As the movement gained ground in the 1970s, news reporters constantly quizzed WMU officers. Marie Mathis and Alma Hunt acknowledged that the movement would have its effect on WMU and on Southern Baptist women. One reporter concluded that while militant churchwomen in some denominations were "storming the pulpits . . . other soft-spoken women are following a circuitous route to high church positions." Mathis said, "Don't think we're not progressive." Hunt added, "We're just not militant."

As women took employment outside the home, WMU membership and participation declined, especially for adults. WMU made major program adjustments to fit the schedules of modern women and children. They also initiated an enlistment drive called Giant Step in 1972. Through these efforts, the falling numbers stabilized in 1974. Enrollment remained stable for several years.

At the 1974 Annual Meeting, Alma Hunt said in her retirement address, "I believe Woman's Missionary Union lifts a woman's perspective above the kitchen sink, or above the desk, or above the industry where she works to see a world in need and to see that she herself can have a part in it. I believe that WMU enables women to be molders of circumstances rather than victims of circumstances."[1]

Carolyn Weatherford, who succeeded Hunt in 1974, decided WMU officials should give serious attention to the movement, as it was becoming increasingly controversial and affecting its members. At WMU's invitation, the Christian Life Commission conducted a seminar on Freedom for Christian Women at the 1975 Executive Board meeting. This was a study of biblical and current views. Meanwhile, WMU publications looked at various aspects of women's roles, reflecting the ambivalent feeling of most Southern Baptists.

One way WMU tried to expand its membership was with coed programs. Beginning in 1977, WMU produced books suggesting activities for one-day missions education experiences. These were aimed at couples, the entire church membership, families, and other groups that might involve persons not previously reached with missions education.

Emmanuel McCall, of the Home Mission Board (HMB), and Carolyn Weatherford agreed that WMU, SBC, needed an African American staff member to further work in African American churches. The HMB provided funding, and in 1978, Margaret Thomas Perkins became the first African American to serve on the professional staff of WMU. Perkins invited key African American WMU leaders and pastors to Birmingham in 1980 to discuss expansion of WMU in African American churches. Their efforts were rewarded as more African American women began attending WMU conferences. Perkins worked for nearly 20 years to strengthen missions education and involvement in SBC African American churches.

Hearing the Call

Beyond WMU enrollment, women and missions were suffering another decline in the 1970s; fewer women were entering missions professions. The proportion of women in SBC agencies was declining at the same time that women in the secular labor force were increasing. These trends prompted WMU leadership to search for new ways to encourage women and girls to follow God's call. WMU also worked toward opening more opportunities for women to serve.

WMU magazines began including articles on career missions opportunities for women, explaining in detail the appointment processes. When WMU edited its statement of tasks in the mid-1970s, one of those tasks was to "provide an environment in which persons can hear and respond to God's call to missionary service."

In 1978 WMU and ten SBC agencies cosponsored a Consultation on Women in Church-Related Vocations. WMU's efforts to recruit more women in ministry would be criticized for at least the next decade. Carolyn Weatherford explained that *women in ministry* was a modern phrase for what had been known as *women in church-related vocations.* She said, "The word *minister* doesn't necessarily mean ordination. Each church decides for itself whether or not to ordain specific staff members. WMU always used the word *minister* even for laypersons. WMU's biggest concern is that women not forget missions careers, no matter how many secular and church jobs might open to them. One of WMU's important jobs is to create an environment through which persons can hear and respond to God's call into missions. If WMU is to be honest with girls about listening to God's call, we must be informed and concerned about the problems they encounter."[2]

The years 1977 through 1981 were WMU's years of heaviest emphasis on the call to mission service.

WMU also addressed the missionary call by acknowledging the extensive roles of the missionary wife. Weatherford asked Foreign Mission Board (FMB) officials to identify married women missionaries by their own names. She asked that they be permitted job classifications, if they wished, other than the Home and Church category to which wives were routinely assigned.

By 1978 Weatherford wrote her commendation to the executive staff of the FMB for "taking the giant step of classifying women's positions beyond home and church." She stated, "I am a strong supporter of Christian homes, and I know of no more urgent need for married women missionaries to fulfill. Yet, they are filling many other roles. They, with women everywhere, will rise to call you blessed!"[3]

World Hunger

Although early personal service efforts were often about sharing food with the poor, WMU only confronted hunger on a global level when specific crises arose, usually as a response to war. But famines in the 1970s seemed to reach overwhelming proportions. Each night Americans heard news stories about hungry people on the other side of the world. The nightly news showed footage of horrific hunger in Bangladesh, Cambodia, Ethiopia, and the Sudan. Hunger agencies proliferated and Christian authors spoke out with titles such as *Rich Christians in an Age of Hunger*, by Ronald J. Sider.[4]

Southern Baptists wanted to help, but they preferred giving through their trusted agencies. In 1974 the FMB began to receive hunger relief contributions. At the 1976 WMU Annual Meeting a noonday prayertime was held on behalf of hungry people around the world, and the hunger crisis was featured on the covers of *Royal Service* and *Contempo* that same year. And once again, in July 1978, the magazines devoted their entire issues to the topic. The Brotherhood Commission invited WMU and SBC agencies to form an ad hoc committee to deal with hunger, appointing the Christian Life Commission to take the lead in coordinating agencies' efforts.

Southern Baptists' first World Hunger Day was observed in 1978. A Convocation in World Hunger, including WMU, the FMB, and the Home Mission Board (HMB), and several other SBC agencies, was held in November. State WMU offices got involved by distributing promotional material for World Hunger Day, which later became a fixed event on the denomination's calendar, set for the second Sunday in October.

From the beginning, WMU approached World Hunger Day as an educational, not a money-raising, event. However, local churches gave money, and the agencies agreed to distribute the contributions to the FMB or HMB. In 1974, $299,000 was sent spontaneously to the FMB. By 1985, FMB hunger and disaster contributions grew to $11 million, plus another $1,150,000 was given to the HMB.

WMU's biggest focus on world hunger came during the 1979–82 WMU emphasis on Life-Changing Commitments. Women were encouraged to live more simply so others might eat. In April 1980, women studied

The Woman I Am in a Hungry World, a book and cassette written by Ruth Fowler.

Will You Take Me to Church?

Southern Baptists became increasingly concerned about unchurched children in the 1970s. Falling church attendance, splintered families, and other influences meant many children never attended church. Bus ministries proliferated, with churches bringing children to church without their parents.

These efforts were somewhat successful in the suburbs, but many unchurched children lived in urban areas as well. By 1973, Southern Baptists were moving from the cities to the suburbs and the city churches suffered drastic declines in membership. Some of the churches were sold and others were left to survive on little or no support from former members. An SBC team was formed to study these forgotten churches to plan how they could minister in declining or rapidly changing neighborhoods. WMU responded by creating Big A Clubs and publishing literature for teaching the Bible to children with no previous church background. WMU members and leaders from all areas of the church taught weekday classes to a receptive group of children.

In 1977 Big A Clubs were highly popular with leaders and children alike. The clubs taught simple Bible truths to children who knew poverty and educational limitations. Clubs were held in city parks, backyards, and church basements.

The idea was quite successful with home missionaries, foreign missionaries, individuals—adults and youth—organizing Big A Clubs. Although no statistics were kept on the children reached, more than 20,000 copies of the beginning teacher's book were sold.

New Opportunities for Members

From children to adults, opportunities for WMU members increased during the 1970s. With the new age-level designations that occurred in 1970 to coordinate with the changes in SBC agencies, WMU members were poised to try new things.

Work with the youngest grew during this decade. *Mission Friends Share,* a quarterly packet of take-home pieces for Mission Friends members aged three through five, began in 1978. The material reached 140,000 preschoolers in mission study that year.

Acteens organizations flourished in this decade. The first National Acteens Convention (NAC) was held in 1972 at Glorieta Baptist Conference Center (now LifeWay Conference Center at Glorieta) in New Mexico. Approximately 900 teenage girls and their leaders from across the nation came together to worship, learn, and fellowship. The conventions, which were held every three to four years, were well liked by both the girls and their leaders. By 1979 registration was at 11,500.

In 1977, WMU developed a program that allowed Acteens direct input into their organization. Six girls were chosen annually to serve on the Acteens National Advisory Panel. Panelists served as pages at national WMU Annual Meetings and at Southern Baptist Conventions.

A short-term volunteer missions program, Acteens Activators, was launched in 1976. Teenage girls and their leaders completed at least 50 hours of supervised training before assisting in missions project on the field. Later on, the program extended to international missions work, and continued to grow.

Baptist Young Women had their first national conference, Kaleidoscope, in 1976. It was held in connection with the WMU Annual Meeting and attracted more than 600 young women. In 1977 the young women's organization grew to include college-age women, with groups developing on college campuses at the request of the Sunday School Board's National Student Ministries. Even the United States Military Academy at West Point established a BYW organization.

The Baptist Women organization was hard hit by the 1970s' women's liberation movement and by its own organizational changes. WMU proclaimed 1978–79 as Baptist Women Year in the Church. This major emphasis upgraded the organization's image and started new groups nationwide. The emphasis resulted in 686 new organizations.

Precious in His Sight

From the early beginnings, WMU helped African American women establish missionary societies in their own churches. And, in the 1970s, African American women began joining WMU organizations. In the West and North, African Americans were uniting with Southern Baptist churches and the women were welcomed into WMU organizations. Through these enrollment points, African American women showed up at national conferences and conventions.

As WMU spread geographically, it embraced significant changes in cultural makeup. In 1975, one WMU organization in New York City reported having members from Ceylon, Cuba, Haiti, Congo, Brazil, Panama, Hong Kong, Taiwan, and the US. Having organizations in new areas brought new ideas to WMU. Leaders and members gained a greater understanding of racial openness and respect for people of other cultures.

The national office in Birmingham became a training center for WMU groups of all backgrounds. Key Spanish WMU leaders were invited to Birmingham in 1979 for intensive training. The next year, leading women of a half dozen different ethnic groups visited.

WMU expanded its language materials in 1980 with the first leaflets in Chinese, Japanese, Korean, Romanian, and simplified English. The first piece was a biographical sketch of Lottie Moon, the second piece was a biographical sketch of Annie Armstrong. Next came leaflets in various languages on how to organize and maintain a WMU organization.

Bread and Butter

By the 1970s WMU's special Christmas and Easter offerings had become churchwide traditions and WMU no longer controlled their allocations. However, as the offerings became successful they also attracted some controversies.

Although the offerings brought praise from missionaries, they also evoked criticism from some prominent leaders. Critics thought the offerings threatened the Cooperative Program, perhaps diverting funds away from SBC's bread-and-butter money. The HMB decided to see if this was true and researched the offerings' effects in 1971. They found that churches giving generously to special offerings were also likely to give to the Cooperative Program.

Another challenge to the special offerings emerged as some churches began combining all the special missions offerings into a single offering taken at Christmas, or moved to year-round giving to missions. The plan supposedly gave higher visibility to missions and attracted larger sums of money.

WMU officers thought the combined offering was a terrible idea, and they said so. They went so far as to avoid speaking at churches that were pushing the plan, telling their conference audiences that the combined offerings were just another way to reduce the consistent, repetitive appeal for missions. Extensive research regarding prayer and giving indicated that eliminating the special offerings

Carolyn Weatherford: 1974–89

Life for Carolyn Weatherford as a little girl was citrus and church, but it became leading and loving, as for 15 years she served as WMU's executive director. Born in Mississippi in 1930, she and her family soon moved to Frostproof, Florida, where her father, Rufus, was a citrus grower. Carolyn grew up with one brother, one sister, and 18 cats. Her mother, Doris, enrolled her little ones in every church activity, including Sunbeam Band. When Carolyn was a GA, her mother was the GA leader; and by the time Carolyn was 14, she herself became counselor for GAs just younger than she. A state WMU officer recognized potential in the young girl and arranged for her to attend Ridgecrest Baptist Conference Center in North Carolina when she was 16. At the end of the conference there, Carolyn committed her life to God's service.

Carolyn's church in Frostproof became the workshop where she learned about leadership, Baptists, and missions, as she became involved in responsibilities in a multitude of church ministries.

Missionary service was always at the back of her mind as she finished college and began a 5-year career as a librarian. Still feeling compelled to missions, Carolyn enrolled in New Orleans Baptist Theological Seminary. Many people suggested professional WMU work to her, but ironically, she was not interested. She applied for foreign mission service, but a medical condition prevented her appointment. After that, she worked with GAs in Florida and her appreciation for WMU grew into devotion. Upon the retirement of Alma Hunt in 1974, national WMU tapped Carolyn Weatherford to be the new executive director.

Carolyn Weatherford's management style was unique. She preferred delegating most operational details to a team of executive managers and spending most of her time traveling, speaking, and promoting WMU and it missions challenge. Like her predecessor, she had excellent relationships with the various SBC entity directors and they worked together with a spirit of unity and purpose. One of the national presidents who served with her, Dorothy Sample, said, "Her greatest strength is her ability to like and get along with all people."

Carolyn Weatherford was a prolific writer, and was the first WMU spokeswomen to gain a hearing by way of audio- and videotape. She became "aunt" to scores of college-age missionary kids (MKs), and gave intense support to the Baptist World Alliance. She also served on the boards of a number of denominational agencies.

Carolyn considered herself "the climate" of WMU, gauging the situation in the SBC as she traveled and related to Convention leaders. When controversy had begun swirling in various SBC agencies, Carolyn took as her goal: "Do not get involved in squabbles." The new WMU national headquarters was built during her tenure as executive director, and paid for as well. New Hope Publishers, a WMU imprint, was also born during the Carolyn Weatherford years.

In many of her speeches across the country, Carolyn Weatherford commented: "I'm not married—yet!!" But in 1989, that changed and she became Carolyn Weatherford Crumpler, a pastor's wife in Ohio—now involved in WMU on a different playing field, but still with the same passion and heart for fulfilling God's call to be "on mission" for Him.

Portions from *Laborers Together with God* by Catherine Allen (WMU, 1987).

would reduce missions education and prayer. WMU also believed individuals would give more in two separate appeals than in one. Again, they had the backing of the FMB. Alma Hunt brought the matter before the FMB in October 1971, sharing her "honest conviction that if the offerings are combined the weeks of prayer will ultimately be combined, and we will lose one week of emphasis on missions now well-established in the churches."[5]

To counteract the Texas church's plan, WMU and the HMB staff organized an informal coordination group in 1976 to plan promotion of the Annie Armstrong Easter Offering®. A similar group was formed with the FMB later on. Sunday School Board publications and programs traditionally granted publication space to advertise the weeks of prayer, offering goals, and observances in curriculum materials. Baptist state papers used extensive press kits. However, many churches still prefer to combine all special missions offerings into one single offering.

Christine Burton Gregory: 1975–81

Christine Gregory lent a style all her own to Woman's Missionary Union. Calling herself a "plain woman," she was anything but plain in her success as a teacher among women, becoming a champion of the local woman in the pew. Christine considered herself a traditional woman and was from the traditional state of Virginia, but never permitted herself to be put on a pedestal. Pageantry was not her style. Practicality was. Her belief in missions, soul competency, and local church autonomy were the mainstays of her faith.

Born in Greenville, South Carolina, in 1921, Christine Burton grew up loving missions and GA in her local church. A leader in church and school, she was a top student and debater—becoming president of BSU at Winthrop College. Christine became a schoolteacher in Greenville and continued displaying leadership skills there and in her church. In 1948, the 27-year-old Christine married A. Harrison Gregory, a Clemson University graduate in chemistry, and they moved to Danville, Virginia. In short order, she was asked to be religious education director at First Baptist Church, resigning just prior to the birth of her first son. By 1956, she was the mother of three sons and active in church and community. At 38, Christine became president of her local WMU, giving it her special touch through promotion and originality. Next she became associational director, but never set leadership as a goal, simply being available to what God opened up.

All about her, Christine observed social problems: poverty, racial prejudice, illiteracy. Her concerns soon led her to becoming mission action chairman for Virginia WMU, and in 1971, she was elected state president. Her idea of leadership was not traditional. She felt leaders were servants—called to pray, to think, to take risks if necessary. When asked to be national president in 1975, Christine Gregory insisted she did not fit the mold. When she first took the stage, Christine told the Convention: "Heavens to Betsy! You will have to accept me for what I am: a plain woman, loving missions with all my heart."

Christine had a gift for straightforward administration, planning programs strong in content, not flashy. She did not shirk from injecting strong program content from various viewpoints. Times were turbulent. So were popular issues. Christine Gregory handled them with grace—not pushing her personal opinions but firmly stating: "My subject is missions."

Before her tenure was ended, Christine Gregory had begun the preparation for a new building for WMU and had discovered her hard work to be a joyful experience. And just two days after her retirement as president, she was elected first vice-president of the Southern Baptist Convention, the first woman ever to hold that office. After serving in numerous Baptist leadership positions, she was elected president of the Baptist General Association of Virginia. And yes, she was the first woman to hold this office too.

When the tensions in the SBC in 1985 led to the formation of a peace committee, Christine Gregory was elected a member. Throughout her distinguished service to WMU, and as a Baptist statesperson, Christine Gregory remained true to her faith, to the principles of soul competency, and to the call of the Great Commission.

New Opportunities and New Challenges

The 1970s continued nationwide social changes that had begun a decade earlier. The effects on WMU were wide-ranging. Although membership declined as women took advantage of new opportunities available to them outside the home, more opportunities opened up for women and girls to learn about missions. WMU members of all ages participated in missions education and mission action that led them to a take on a broader view of their nation and their world. Nevertheless, just around the corner, with the dawning of a new decade, SBC waters were churning. Changes in viewpoints would challenge the very foundation of Woman's Missionary Union. But that foundation was built on the Rock.

12
1981–1990

Challenges—changes—trends—confronted Woman's
Missionary Union on every hand as the new decade
began, and women focused with oneness of heart on their
goal of living out the Great Commission. Carolyn
Weatherford's final report to the WMU Executive Board
reflected this unity of purpose: "Again and again the
WMU Executive Board has expressed its determination to
retain the singular purposes of missions. . . . Without
apology, we can move into the 80s aggressively, seeking to
enroll more women, more girls, more preschoolers in
missions participation."[1]

Reinforcing women's resolve to keep centered on missions, Weatherford challenged those at the 1980 Annual
Meeting in St. Louis to "hold high the torch of missions
until it burns brightly to the ends of the earth."[2]

It was June 1981. At the WMU Annual Meeting in
Los Angeles, Dorothy Sample was elected national president, bringing to that office years of WMU experience
and training, plus skills in theology and psychology. The
talents and spirit of all WMU constituency would be challenged and honed by the changes presented during this
new decade. Some changes were good, some were
needed, some were frustrating, and many were inevitable.
All demanded the talents and spirit that are a hallmark of
the women of WMU.

Dorothy Elliott Sample: 1981–86

She was born in a little mining town in Alabama in 1938, but Dorothy "Dot" Elliott ended up in a pioneer Southern Baptist area, Michigan. The young Dot was a Sunbeam; but when her family moved to a Free Will Baptist church, she missed out on GA. As a college coed in Nashville, Dot met Richard Sample. The two of them graduated in 1961; Dot was valedictorian and Richard, salutatorian. They married that summer and moved to Michigan. Both continued in higher education, eventually earning master's and doctor's degrees in theology and raising a family at the same time. Dot's doctoral dissertation was an investigation of what Baptists had done to fulfill the Great Commission, certainly fitting, considering the plans God had in mind for this brilliant woman.

The Samples felt the call to missions and applied for appointment, hoping to teach in a seminary in Asia. That was not possible, as Dot was diagnosed with a rare genetic disease. Through treatment, she regained fairly good health, but overseas service was no longer an option.

The Samples committed themselves to developing Southern Baptist churches in Michigan. In addition to nurturing three children, Dot completed yet another doctor's degree, this one in psychology and administration. All the time, this spirited woman was deeply involved in WMU activities. Through her involvement, she was galvanized by the principle that no matter what demands were on her time, her life, she could "stand in the gap" as God opened doors. She was a popular speaker and conference leader and held one WMU position after another before being elected Michigan WMU president in 1978.

As well as her job with WMU, and working as an innovative teacher, Dot Sample somehow found time to maintain a private counseling practice. Then, to compound a more-than-full schedule, she was selected national WMU president in 1981. Only Fannie Heck had become national president at a younger age. Dot brought unique skills to the position and motivated WMU leaders to be involved in missions and, at the same time, minister to personal needs. With her diverse skills, Dot was able to make an impact on many levels. Very likely, she was called upon to do more traveling than any national president in WMU's history. In her 5 years as president, she had two major surgeries, causing her son Scott to comment, "Mom, you live yourself to death."

Dot Sample was instrumental in urging WMU into video production for training and WMU promotion and was involved in the project of a new headquarters for WMU. She found this one of the highlights of her tenure. The national staff grew during her years, and she led in a restructuring of the Executive Board.

Dot was a dynamic advocate for women, realizing their talents, their places, and their responsibilities in fulfilling the Great Commission. This was a difficult period in the SBC. However, WMU purposely led meetings emphasizing love, unity, and a spirit of hope. Dot's tenure ended in 1986, but her involvement in WMU, in unique ministries, in touching lives, continued unabated. Dot Sample loved to speak on the idea of "finding one's life by losing it." Her favorite motto? Plan well and don't worry.

Portions from *Laborers Together with God* by Catherine Allen (WMU, 1987).

New Hope

An immediate challenge was office space for national headquarters. Growth had again led to overcrowding and national leadership looked to more and varied future needs as they contemplated action. Planning began in 1981, and by September of the next year, WMU had purchased 25 acres of land and plans were approved for a new headquarters. Even the name lent a positive note, for WMU's new home would be on top of New Hope Mountain, south of Birmingham, Alabama, and the address was 100 Missionary Ridge. Many WMU staff members, Executive Board members, and countless interested WMU women poured hours of work and dedication into the new 137,000-square-foot facility. It included offices, library, conference space, warehouse, and publishing facilities, and was set off by a beautiful lobby, featuring a unique global fountain and missions displays from across the years and around the world. A highlight of the display is Lottie Moon's trunk and oriental artifacts.

Tucked beneath the cornerstone is a copper-lined vault holding historical information about WMU.

States and individuals were invited to donate designated amounts that would allow them to name an area of the building. These areas were then decorated reflecting the country, area, or person thus honored. Temporarily funded by a loan, financing the building of the new headquarters was the first time in its history that WMU had requested money for its own purposes. WMU did not stage a fund-raising campaign, but the money came in. Amazingly, by 1988 WMU's beautiful new building was completely paid for.[3] Only eternity can know of the dedication and skill of leading WMU members who helped the dream become fact. Catherine Allen, associate executive director, was doubtless the central figure in bringing the dream to reality. Staff moved in on May 28, 1984,[4] and 100 Missionary Ridge was formally dedicated on January 16, 1985.[5]

Print Plus

In facing new challenges in the decade, WMU continued to look for new ways of telling the old story. It had been 80 years since the fledgling missions literature department had, in 1906, daringly invested about $1,500 in literature. By the beginning of the 1980s, WMU had built its sales to $8 million and had distributed a half billion pages of literature.

The initial magazine for women, *Our Mission Fields,* was first published in 1906; it was renamed *Royal Service* in 1914, and went by that name for more than 80 years. In 1984, it was made available on tape for the visually impaired. Two years earlier, *Our Missions World,* a magazine with vocabulary geared for hearing impaired readers and people just learning to read English, began publication.[6]

WMU began "publishing" through video in 1982, starting with tapes for leadership training. The new headquarters building had been engineered as a telecommunications base. They were licensed to transmit to satellite, and had space for a television studio. By 1985, WMU was selling videotaped mission study aids and helped SBC missions agencies produce programs of the Sunday School Board's BTN network.

WMU was the pacesetter among Southern Baptists videoing conferences, working with the boards to sponsor five conferences by 1986. The single largest conference had 12,000 viewers in live audiences in nearly 400 sites.

This video trend was not the only drawing card for WMU women, however. During 1984–85 alone, more than 85,000 women attended WMU state and national conventions and conferences.

Another New

With the new WMU building sitting atop New Hope Mountain, an appropriate follow-through of the concept was New Hope Publishers—WMU's new imprint, which published unique missions education products. Initiated in 1985, many New Hope publications were books on content or methods of teaching missions, some of which were produced in cooperation with the Foreign Mission Board (FMB). The imprint also provided missions literature for an audience not necessarily a part of WMU, opening an avenue to reach all Christian women. Some publications were geared to casual readers, others to new parents, and yet others to youth. They introduced topics with wide appeal to an audience never before reached by WMU. The new imprint tried new methods of distribution including direct marketing and selling through bookstores.

The New Ethnic Outreach

WMU took on a new look in cultures and colors with the growth of ethnic outreach. Involvement with Spanish-speaking persons dated back to 1888 with Mina Everett. She was followed by several leaders in Texas who worked with Hispanics. The ministry blossomed in the 1970s when Guatemala-born Doris Diaz, a Home Mission Board (HMB) worker who was editor of *Nuestra Tarea,* moved to WMU headquarters. The remarkable Diaz exhibited her heart for the world when she became language consultant specialist for other ethnic-language groups in addition to Hispanics, encouraging and involving women of many cultures from New York to California.[7]

And in this decade, as WMU organizations expanded into new states, ethnic groups began to grow at a faster rate than Anglos. By 1986 the number of African American churches in the SBC had grown to around 1,000, and more than 50,000 African Americans were members of largely Anglo churches. Emmanuel McCall, HMB's director of Black Church Relations, advised pioneering churches to "start a WMU at the same time you start Sunday School." McCall declared, "In most instances, WMUs have prodded men in other denominational structures to take seriously racial reconciliation and interracial ministry." He viewed WMU as a strategy for developing healthy churches committed to missions.

WMU organizations sprang up around the world as well. The earliest had been Brazil in 1908, and, according to a 1986 survey, 58 countries related to Southern Baptist missions now had nationwide women's organizations. At least 47 of these followed the WMU, SBC, plan, 38 of them using the traditional WMU emblem and 39 adopting the same motto. Another first for WMU history in the United States occurred at the 1988 Annual Meeting when several of the major addresses were simultaneously presented in both English and Spanish.[8]

New Growth—New Trends

A not-so-new trend became stronger in the 1980s, as more and more women joined the workforce. Naturally, the traditional daytime WMU activities were inaccessible to working women and additional evening meetings were often not an option for those with an already overcrowded schedule. STARTEAM, a national enlargement plan, was implemented in 1980, and in a 3-year period, more than 3,000 churches started some kind of missions work. WMU membership reflected an increase in every age-level organization. By 1984, there was a slight drop in the net number of members, but an increase in total WMU organization membership.[9]

By the end of the decade, Weatherford reported that membership in WMU was leveling out. The 1989 Annual Report showed total membership at slightly more than 1,200,000.[10] Without doubt, the challenge of finding new ways to share the missions message continued into the next decade.

Another trend was the steady growth of the Lottie Moon Christmas Offering® (LMCO℠) and Annie Armstrong Easter Offering® (AAEO℠). They demonstrated an astounding ability to thrive, no matter what the economic climate. WMU has been amazingly successful in inspiring the constituency to mission support. Seemingly, as women read Catherine Allen's *The New Lottie Moon Story* and Bobbie Sorrill's in-depth *Annie Armstrong: Dreamer in Action* giving increased. At the 1981 Annual Meeting, Carolyn Weatherford announced the 1980 total for the LMCO as exceeding $44,000,000. By the end of the decade, the LMCO had grown to $50,197,870, and the AAEO stood at 39,993,023.[11]

New approaches were instigated in WMU youth organizations during the decade. Girls in Action's Missions Adventures (which had replaced Forward Steps

Marjorie McCullough: 1986–91

 *Uniquely gifted.* What an apt term for Marjorie Jones McCullough. A Louisiana girl, Marjorie was born in 1924, and grew up in WMU children's organizations. Even as a teenager, she was initiating ministries across racial barriers, a real trailblazer. She knew early on that she wanted to be a missionary. After college, Marjorie attended WMU Training School in Louisville, and with her master's degree came her introduction to professional WMU work. She worked with several state WMUs directing various youth organizations. She was actually on the committee that decided to turn RA work over to the Brotherhood Commission.

All of her missions involvement led Marjorie to a renewed sense of her calling, and she was appointed a missionary to Nigeria in 1955. Although Marjorie was a teacher, WMU work in Nigeria was her real passion. She understudied Neale Young, the pioneer WMU leader in that nation. Then Marjorie was asked to move to Ghana as director of WMU work, holding that pioneer role for 8 years and learning still another language.

While on furlough in 1964, national WMU asked her to become director of Girls' Auxiliary. Marjorie became a key figure in creating and giving new names to two age-level organizations: Acteens and Girls in Action. It was Marjorie who wrote the new manual and handbook for Acteens.

Brazil wanted Marjorie to come to their 20th anniversary celebration of GA in 1969. The renewed challenge of hands-on foreign missions captured her heart anew, and by August 1969, she was again a foreign missionary, this time in Brazil. She set out to learn yet another language—Portuguese. Again she trained WMU leaders and wrote literature, realizing afresh how alike at heart are the world's women of WMU.

On furlough in 1972–73, Marjorie attended the Southern Baptist Convention and ran into an old friend, Glendon McCullough, newly elected director of the Brotherhood Commission. He was widowed and the father of four children. Marjorie returned to Brazil with a marriage proposal to consider. They married in 1977 and lived in Tennessee. Marjorie Jones McCullough found herself an instant mother to teens and preteens. But in a shockingly short time, the world turned over again when Glendon McCullough was killed when his car was struck by a drunk driver. Marjorie legally adopted the four children.

In 1980, Marjorie was selected Tennessee WMU president,

and in 1986 she was asked to be national president. Her key goal became guiding WMU in keeping its missions emphasis and vision. She was part of the first group to make a Lottie Moon tour of China, and made a total of four such heritage trips. WMU's Centennial was a high point during her years as president, and the Second Century Fund was established during her tenure.

This superbly gifted woman with a heart shaped by missions sensed the importance of the past in looking to the future. She stated emphatically: "I don't think we need to always do things like they did in the past, but we *do* need to remember who we are and where we came from and what it took to get us where we are today."

Marjorie McCullough died on March 18, 2006, following a lengthy illness; however, her vision for a future filled with bright hope continues to motivate WMU leadership and members.

Portions from *Laborers Together with God* by Catherine Allen (WMU, 1987).

in 1970) was redesigned in 1988, but retained the goal of learning about the Bible, missions, and being a Baptist. In similar fashion, Acteens' StudiAct was redesigned and updated in the same year. The decade ended with the fourth National Acteens Convention held in San Antonio, Texas, and attended by an amazing number of teenage girls—13,600.[12]

WMU's annual conferences at Ridgecrest and Glorieta continued to draw many women who came for inspiration, training, and fellowship. Ridgecrest had more in attendance, but both were consistently well attended, with numbers of participants ranging from 1,200 to 2,500 or more. In 1982, WMU partnered with the HMB in sponsoring the first national evangelistic conference for women, Dayspring. A total of more than 5,000 women attended the Daysprings at Ridgecrest and in Fort Worth, Texas.

Near the end of the decade, WMU joined the SBC's Missions Education Council in organizing Jericho. This was a missions conference held both at Ridgecrest and

Glorieta, providing an interactive, family-friendly missions experience for laypersons. These conferences replaced the traditional Foreign Missions Weeks. Highlights of Jericho varied from the popular afternoon missions fair to dramas and hands-on projects. Church members learned new approaches to missions and took these ideas home to share with churches across the Convention.

Jericho conferences kept on training and inspiring a diversity of church members for nearly a decade, producing new missionaries and strengthening mission support from the home base. It was also a successful example of how SBC entities could work together.

The New and the Continuing

The 1980s for WMU presented diverse challenges and fresh opportunities. The event of the decade was the celebration of WMU's first 100 years. Indeed, there was much to celebrate. A 100-year survey of purposes showed WMU's remarkable steadiness of purpose. WMU's unde-viating goal? Support missions through prayer, giving, and doing. It is a fact that this organization unlocked essen-tially every door that is now open for women in Southern Baptist life. This, however, was never WMU's purpose—but simply a by-product of an amazingly efficient organi-zation. One founding member said at that first meeting in 1888: "To say that this is a woman's rights movement is absurd." Nevertheless, history has shown that women *did* gain a platform.

WMU's first century reflects a body of women gaining influence through proven excellence in organization and administration. By the 1980s, the WMU Executive Board was meeting twice a year, developing missions programs for local churches and associations. Elected board officials and state WMU professionals represented all age groups and members. They consistently solicited input from SBC agencies in order to further facilitate cooperation and effectiveness.

By the time of the Centennial celebration, the national WMU office had more than 100 employees. Following the trends of American society, a large percentage of WMU's professionals were married and a number had small children. And at least 10 percent of the workforce was male. The leaders of WMU were a true cross section of America—well-to-do, poor, middle-class, ethnically diverse, from many backgrounds and from varied geographic areas.

Women chose as their Centennial theme: A Century to Celebrate, a Future to Fulfill.[13] Commemorative issues of the WMU magazines were prepared and lent an authentic touch of the past to the gathering.[14]

An air of excitement and thanksgiving permeated the Centennial sessions meeting in Richmond, Virginia, exactly 100 years from the day those 32 delegates and some 200 more women met in the same city to found Woman's Missionary Union, Auxiliary to Southern Baptist Convention. Would they not be astounded to see what God had done in those 100 years? Here was WMU, meeting to celebrate the dedication and commitment of those pioneer leaders—a meeting that registered 10,947 participants.[15] Former national president Christine Gregory recalls the excitement of that historic gathering. She considers it amazing, the "proof that an organization could survive 100 years—still fueled by prayer, a shoestring budget, and singleness of purpose in carrying out the Great Commission." She remembers Richmond filled with women, many from across the world, and an air of exhilaration combined with an extraordinary sense of camaraderie.[16]

By this Centennial year, WMU had contributed more than $1 billion to missions. That did not even include local and state missions giving. A trail of sacrificial giving and a devotion to purpose led back to thousands of unsung heroes who had saved egg money and tucked away needed pennies and dimes in a sugar bowl sitting on a shelf. And the women gathered in Richmond in 1988 gave thanks for their WMU predecessors who had invested their hearts and their pocketbooks in saving the mission boards from total collapse, and recalled how women had financed Baptist expansion into 50 states and more than 100 countries. All this had occurred in a mere 100 years—marked as they were by wars, poverty, and change.

WMU's unique Second Century Fund was built as a permanent memorial to this Centennial celebration, honoring those who had invested their lives and hearts to missions. Enabling the development of women leaders, its purpose was to give special attention to women's organizations in new, developing Baptist areas in the United States and around the world. And the fund has continued to thrive in subsequent years.[17]

New Frontiers of Involvement

The Second Century Fund was just one of several new approaches to meeting needs that were instigated during this decade. Baptist Nursing Fellowship[SM] (BNF®) was organized in 1983 and provided nurses and nursing students opportunities for worship and witnessing through becoming personally involved in home and international missions ministries.[18] By the end of the 1980s, there were already 969 members in 23 state organizations.[19]

At the same time WMU was reaching out in new ways to further its purpose of mission support and involvement, conflicts were sweeping throughout the Southern Baptist Convention. Every entity among Southern Baptists was affected by change and controversy. The issues were many, but included the interpretation of Scripture, questionable theology in SBC seminaries, how to go about social ministries, the role of women in ministry including ordination. Contention swirled around one issue after another.

A real source of contention was WMU as *auxiliary*. It became increasingly evident that those gaining control of the SBC wanted WMU to become an agency of the Convention. WMU as an auxiliary had historically proven their success at promoting the great missions offerings and at the same time serving as leaders in "stimulating the missionary spirit" in comprehensive missions education in the churches. The questions were legion. In the midst of debate and sometimes even threats, WMU as a body determined to, as much as possible, focus on their mission and at the same time remain relevant and committed to the overarching purpose of promoting missions.[20] The vote of WMU's Executive Board was unanimous as they agreed to retain their historic auxiliary status.[21]

At the same time, the relationship of WMU with state Baptist organizations remained solid. WMU leaders learned to work with all segments for the purpose of missions, striving to continue their vital work unabated.

At the 1988 WMU Annual Meeting, Weatherford pointedly asked key questions: "What is our purpose? To what will we give our support? What will WMU fight for if necessary? It is not a struggle over rights of Southern Baptist women. Rather, it is the right and responsibility of every Southern Baptist woman to serve her Lord through the fundamentals of WMU."[22] Throughout this turbulent decade, WMU leadership had decided to "stick to our knitting" and keep to the fundamental goals.[23]

In 1989, in Carolyn Weatherford's final report to the WMU Annual Meeting at the time of her retirement, she reflected on the changes in the SBC during her 15 years as executive director, recalling that in 1976, denominational cooperation had been at its peak. However, 1989 presented a very different picture. Nevertheless, Weatherford noted that "nothing that divides us is as important as that which binds us to Christ's mandate to go into all the world and preach the gospel to all the people."[24]

WMU ended one decade and began another with a new executive director, a widely experienced and highly talented woman who had served as a missionary in Indonesia. Elected as sixth executive director of WMU in 1989, Dellanna O'Brien determined to lead the women of WMU into the decade, confident that the mandate to accept the challenge of the Great Commission had not changed. Steadfastly, Southern Baptist women committed themselves to following Christ's command to go into all the world. They could not know the future, but the blood of those pioneer women flowed in their veins. The spirit of those courageous ancestors would inspire their continued service into a new millennium.

13
1991–2000

A new director. A new president. A new determination to continue the founding goal of mission support that had prompted their organization more than a century before. WMU began the final decade of the millennium with newness. It was a decade marked by change and stability, challenge and consistency, innovation and vision.

A Decade of Innovation

WMU ministries in the 1990s were marked with imaginative ways to enlist, undergird, and encourage Baptist women, youth, and children. The Image Campaign sought to tell a new audience of women about WMU. Advertisements were placed in several magazines including *SBC Life* and regional issues of five national magazines. It also gave longtime WMU members a fresh look at what their organization was doing.[1]

In 1991, the Missionary Housing Office successfully completed its first full year of assisting missionary families with housing while on stateside assignment. Over and over again, families looking for temporary "roots" while in America have thanked WMU for connecting them with a home.[2]

WMU Envisioning the Vision

A pivotal undertaking began in 1992 when president Carolyn Miller appointed The Committee, a group of 17 leaders, to undertake a study of WMU. Their task was to look at WMU's future.[3] Although the Committee was large, they met frequently and did in-depth research, which was followed by countless hours of discussion and prayer. The Committee developed a vision statement and six core values.

WMU's Executive Board approved various recommendations for carrying out the vision in coming years. In 1997 the values were simplified but remained the same in essence. One or two core values brought censure from other agencies, but the unanimity of the entire Executive Board of WMU was remarkable.

Vision Statement and Core Values developed by The Committee

Vision Statement:
Woman's Missionary Union exists to enable churches and believers to participate in introducing all persons in the world to Christ.

Core Values:
1. We affirm and uphold the "priesthood of the believer," while accepting the responsibilities and privileges inherent therein.
2. We acknowledge God's call to every believer to carry the good news of Jesus Christ to all the world.
3. We recognize, emphasize, and affirm the giftedness of women and girls in Christian endeavors.
4. We acknowledge the biblical mandate to respond to social and moral issues with actions as modeled by Jesus Christ and with a message of His redemptive plan.
5. We acknowledge and accept the responsibility for developing missions leaders.
6. We covenant to partner with Christians around the world, as individually and corporately we multiply each others' efforts to lead a lost world to Christ.[4]

An Organization at Work

Although affected by general social change, and especially by skepticism and sometimes downright animosity from within some SBC entities, WMU's work in megacities outpaced the rest of the nation. WMU grew faster in these cities than the national average, with help from the Mega Focus Cities project. WMU provided training for associational WMU leaders to help them customize a workable program for churches in these vast cities.[5]

Not everyone was opposed to WMU, and often the women found support in surprising ways. In May 1993, an unexpected visit to national WMU was a shot of inspiration. President and Mrs. Jimmy Carter came to see national headquarters and to offer their support and affirmation. The Carters greeted the employees who had gathered in the lobby. This special visit boosted morale and left a long-lasting sense of encouragement.[6]

Resource Renovations

During the decade, people in churches requested missions resources for groupings of children (boys and girls), and many of the requests were from churches without missions organizations. So, in 1991 WMU began making plans to produce coed resources for youth ministry. The first coed products for youth were released under the World Changers Resources imprint and were prepared in cooperation with the Brotherhood Commission.[7] The joint approach presented some difficulties, and in a few years the two developed separate materials with Brotherhood using the World Changers name and WMU using worldfriends press.

More literature updates were in the offing. In 1995, *Contempo,* the Baptist Young Women (BYW) magazine and *Royal Service,* that grand old lady of WMU missions materials, were discontinued and born anew as a combined publication, *Missions Mosaic.* And new names and materials didn't stop there. *Discovery* remained the magazine for younger GAs, and *GA World* was created for older GAs.[8]

Carolyn Miller: 1991–96

 Carolyn Downes and big sister Gwen made a mess of their backyard. They dug. They dug. They dug some more—digging to get to China. The hole was never deep enough, but their hearts were. Gwen Downes (Reece) became a career missionary to Nigeria and little sister Carolyn became president of one of the largest protestant women's missions organization in the world, as her heart encompassed that world in her passion for missions.

Born in Boaz, Alabama, in 1937, Carolyn was nurtured in faith by her mother, Gladys, and her pastor's wife and GA leader, Annie Nelson. Both women passed on their commitment to mission service.

Carolyn's love for missions continued to grow with the passing of years and as she watched her sister leave for mission service in Nigeria. First at the University of Montevallo and then at Auburn University, Carolyn was active in BSU and publicly committed her life to whatever God had in mind.

Her WMU involvement has literally been lifelong, from childhood on. After marriage to Jerry Miller, and busy with three children, Carolyn participated and led in WMU organizations in her home church, First Baptist of Huntsville. Her involvement was associational as well as local and then on to the state level, where she was elected state president two times.

Then in 1991, national WMU tapped Carolyn as its 15th president. Declaring emphatically that her gift was not "speaking," she became an inspiration to thousands of women as she spoke literally hundreds of times. Carolyn was a gifted administrator and relished the opportunity to utilize these skills in touching countless lives during her five years as president.

Carolyn Miller thrived on being able to minister to needs around the world, and rejoiced to be able to serve with a superb executive director like Dellanna O'Brien.

In spite of the manifest difficulties of working through Southern Baptist Convention relationships during such strenuous years, Carolyn was encouraged by evidence of growth through new WMU ministries. Although overall growth did not occur, new organizations continued to spring up, especially in pioneer areas. She was further heartened by the strong programs "born" during her tenure and the way they have continued to grow and change lives.

The challenge of the 1990s was to keep WMU to its task of prayer, teaching, giving, and supporting missions. During her tenure, Carolyn and other WMU leaders determined to focus *not* on Convention controversy, but on their God-given task.

Leaving office in 1996, Carolyn Miller has remained deeply involved in promoting WMU and its challenging programs. She is still "digging her way to the world" as she continues to focus on the task of sharing the good news.

Organizational Adaptations

The new look in magazines accompanied revisions and innovations in WMU's core organizations. A Mission Friends consultant was added to national staff, and Missions Adventures was revised; then in 1997, it became WorldVentures[SM].[9] This same year, the Sunbeam Centennial was highlighted in state and national meetings throughout the Convention.[10] The next year, WMU launched a Web site (www.wmu.com), including interactive pages for all ages.[11] Acteens® expanded their Activators program; and in 1993, over 1,500 teenage girls participated in the program.[12] Four years later, the Acteens individual achievement plan, StudiAct, changed to MissionsQuest[SM].[13]

WMU officially introduced coed organizations in 1995. Children in Action[SM], Youth on Mission[SM], and Adults on Mission[SM] provided plans for all ages in the church. This was also the year that Baptist Young Women and Baptist Women combined to form Women on Mission®, a major step in seeking to define Woman's Missionary Union. At the same time, WMU also presented a plan for simplification of WMU officers for the local church. The intent? To make the structure both less complicated *and* more effective. WMU is the umbrella organization and Women on Mission the component made up of Baptist women involved in mission support.[14]

Decade of Innovation

WMU consistently envisioned and then developed projects to meet needs by involving women in promoting missions.

Baptist Nursing Fellowship℠ (BNF®) celebrated its tenth anniversary in 1993, and started an overseas network.[15] A high point for BNF came when one of their own, Wanda Lee, was elected national WMU president in 1996.

Long-range planning initiated in 1993 led to several more innovations. Volunteer Connection®, one such successful venture, is a resource that connects missions volunteers with needs. In 1996, the program hired its first coordinator, and the following year, WMU joined with Habitat for Humanity in recruiting and processing volunteers.[16] A variety of challenging projects now come under the Volunteer Connection umbrella, including Acteens Activators; Pure Water, Pure Love℠; WorldCrafts℠; and Christian Women's Job Corps® (CWJC®).[17]

Beginning in 1992, WMU partnered with the Home Mission Board (now North American Mission Board) and seven state conventions in the Mississippi River Ministry (MRM). WMU volunteers join Baptists in the seven-state area in building bridges of hope, doing everything from Bible clubs to fixing roofs and providing free health and dental care.

Examples of what God is doing through the Mississippi River Ministry (MRM) abound. Rough and foul-mouthed Nina owned a bar before God touched her life and a miraculous transformation occurred. Now she is a beacon of hope, serving as head of a statewide food distribution ministry. There are many more stories just like Nina's. The MRM has untold numbers of Ninas and Georges and Marys and Tims who now distribute the new hope of God's love.

Reported by Sandy Wisdom-Martin and Gail Pietsrup, Clinic Directors; East St. Louis, Mississippi, March 21, 2005.

Success Story

The concept of Christian Women's Job Corps was born in 1993 and has become a shining example of inspired and effective ministry. Out of observing a crying need to help women break out of the poverty cycle by developing marketable skills, CWJC sprang to life as a way of introducing women to Christ as well. By 1996, four pilot programs were launched: York County Christian Women's Job Corps in South Carolina; San Antonio Christian Women's Job Corps in Texas; Bismarck Christian Women's Job Corps in North Dakota; and Uptown Christian Women's Job Corps in Illinois. Christian women are serving as coordinators, mentors, instructors, and a broad spectrum of related volunteer positions to meet the needs of women at their point of need. Key elements are Bible study, mentoring, skills training, courses in job interviewing, and needed assistance in obtaining a GED or other entry-level job requirements.

CWJC became a permanent program of WMU in March 1997, attesting to its phenomenal success. By the end of the 1990s, there were 115 CWJC job sites in 29 states.[18]

Another Winner—WorldCrafts

WorldCrafts got its start in the backyard of a creative missionary in Thailand who wanted to help desperately needy women be able to support themselves and their children. As the women gathered to make marketable handcraft items, missionaries were able to share God's love with them. Artisans lacked an avenue for selling their products on a broad scale. WorldCrafts was born as a way to tell Southern Baptists a new story. Through this program, artisans are paid for their work when they provide the products, and WorldCrafts markets them in the US. In 1996, WorldCrafts debuted its home party concept, with 12 parties held in the homes of Women on Mission members. By the next year, with publicity and support from Alabama WMU, nearly 100 parties were held. That same year, several leading Christian women's magazines featured the project.[19] By the fall of 1999, the product line included 107 unique items from 16 areas of the world, and 3 more countries joined in that same year.[20]

Pure Water, Pure Love

WMU accepted the administration of Pure Water, Pure Love in 1997 when it transferred from the Brotherhood Commission. This program to helps missionaries secure pure, safe drinking water. WMU provides both filters and water purification equipment. In many areas, water purification is absolutely essential to for the health and well-being of missionaries and those with whom they work. Pure Water, Pure Love enables missionaries to live among unreached peoples in hopes of taking the living water of Christ to them.[21]

Project HELP

A new approach for ministry directed at national social issues came in 1993. Project HELP provided a way for WMU to target a specific social issue for concentrated study and action.[22] Project HELP topics have included hunger, AIDS, cultural diversity, literacy, and restorative justice. In 2004–2006, Project HELP focused on poverty.

Feedback from women across the nation was resoundingly positive regarding the importance of these projects and the end result of blessed and changed lives. Such response encourages national WMU to continue innovative strategies in pinpointing and addressing deep-felt social needs in America.

New to the 1990s

Along with ongoing ministries and new projects, the decade saw significant events. In February 1998, the first TEL (Training Effective Leaders) event was offered, and more than 300 state consultants were trained.

Language work expanded in 1994 when WMU enlisted ten volunteer consultants to serve on a first-ever national WMU Ethnic Advisory Council, further strengthening a growing ministry to various ethnic groups in the US.[23]

And at the next January Board Meeting, WMU dedicated the Alma Hunt Museum, honoring the remarkable woman who had led WMU as executive director for 26 years. The unique collection in the museum, housed in the WMU national headquarters building, interprets and enhances the understanding and appreciation of the contributions WMU has made to the cause of missions.[24]

The diverse talents of the organization's staff was reemphasized when, in 1996, WMU produced a video documentary on hunger, *One Common Need*. It was selected for broadcast on the 13th annual World Food Day Teleconference and won a number of national awards for outstanding production.[25]

Innovators

The WMU Executive Board decided in 1997 to field test a strategy for missions innovators. This program would be coordinated by the national office in conjunction with state organizations to assist individuals, churches, associations, and states in meaningful, innovative approaches to missions involvement. The next year, three staff members were deployed to begin Innovators involvement, strengthening both local and state groups.[26]

Long-Range for Long-Term Leadership

The Christian Women's Leadership Center (CWLC) was established in 2000 as a partnership with Samford University and WMU. Carol Ann Vaughn was the first CWLC director. The CWLC provides learning opportunities for women to realize the fullest measure of their gifts in all areas of human endeavor. With Carver School no longer in operation, CWLC is a strategic place for women to prepare for leadership roles in church, social institutions, government, and the wider marketplace.[27]

A major component of the leadership program is the Eleanor F. Terry Chair for Christian Women's Leadership.

The lead gift was made by Bob Terry, editor of the *Alabama Baptist,* to memorialize his wife because of her passion to train women for leadership. She died from injuries sustained in an automobile accident while attending a council meeting of the Baptist World Alliance.[28]

Vision and a Firm Foundation

Visionary women created the Second Century Fund in 1988 in honor of WMU's first 100 years. This fund is a permanent endowment for developing women's work for missions throughout the world. Each year, projects across the nation and in other countries are funded through this program.

Then in 1993, the WMU Executive Board approved the establishment of the WMU Vision Fund to help finance operations at national WMU office and to fund missions activities not financed through other channels.[29] Each year during the 1990s, the Vision Fund grew and became a conduit for funding thriving missions ministries.

January 1995 ushered in the establishment of the WMU Foundation. Its chief purposes are to support national missions projects of WMU, plus other programs, in order to assure the financial security of WMU.[30] A board of ten trustees named Richard Carnes as the first president of the Foundation in 1995. The WMU Foundation became responsible for overseeing the Vision Fund and various WMU scholarships. The success of the Foundation in its early years exceeded expectations and exhibited great promise for the future.

Preparation for the New Millennium

The decade had begun with a new executive director. Dellanna O'Brien was the sixth director in a line of distinguished and noteworthy women, each a pioneer in her own right. O'Brien spent a decade leading Southern Baptist women and contributing her many talents and skills in dynamic leadership. Administrator, speaker, writer, friend, she left her special heart for missions as a continuing inspiration to women around the world. O'Brien and national president Carolyn Miller guided WMU through some challenging years. Then in 1996, Wanda Lee was elected national president and exceptional leadership continued unabated.

Throughout the 1990s, state and national leadership alike realized that the organization stood at a crucial and pivotal point in its more-than-100-year history. Difficulties were nothing new, however. When viewed historically, WMU was born with intense labor pains. Women persisted in striving for their right to exist in order to fulfill their call to missions. In 1888, they calmly accepted the decision of the men of SBC leadership that WMU not be considered an agency. Instead, they were permitted to organize as an auxiliary, fully assisting the denomination in every possible way to respond to the Great Commission. Then, more than 100 years later, their auxiliary status was challenged, as the SBC made numerous efforts to see WMU become an agency of the Convention and, therefore, under the Convention's control, no longer able to elect their own leadership and promote the agenda they felt to be their missions mandate.

For more than a century, the SBC and WMU had been cooperatively intertwined. And the WMU of the 1990s made deliberate efforts to keep missions above any denominational conflicts and controversies. Consequently, they were determined to remain silent during that critical juncture. Amazingly, in spite of so many Baptists "choosing up sides" and engaging in often bitter dialogue, the women of WMU, from all states and many varying theological and polity perspectives, remained solidly unified in purpose and spirit. Through it all, Woman's Missionary Union never wavered in its goal of

Dellanna O'Brien: 1989–99

From the frontline of missions involvement in Indonesia to WMU headquarters, 10,000 miles away, Dellanna O'Brien was the first international missionary to serve as executive director of Woman's Missionary Union. Selected in 1989, Dellanna directed the course of the organization for a decade.

Dellanna West was born in Wichita Falls, Texas, in 1933. During her freshman year at Hardin-Simmons, Dellanna met Bill O'Brien, and they married in 1952. Ten years later, they went to Indonesia as music missionaries where Dellanna taught piano and English at the seminary in Semarang.

The O'Briens returned to America in 1972 and both worked on graduate studies while Dellanna taught school and Bill pastored a church. After Bill became vice-president of the Foreign Mission Board, Dellanna completed her doctor's degree in education and went on to found International Family and Children's Educational Services, a nonprofit testing service providing help for children of Americans living overseas.

The decade in which she led WMU as chief executive was a turbulent one for Southern Baptists, and her gifts and personal attributes helped immeasurably in keeping the organization focused on its singular goal of missions. Dellanna determined that the conflict seething around WMU would not be divisive within the organization. She worked closely with two national presidents, both with talents and dedication that closely complemented her own, to meet her goal. First Carolyn Miller and then Wanda Lee formed a team with Dellanna through ten years of change and challenge.

A host of effective programs for missions involvement were developed that final decade of the twentieth century, and many of them were due to the keen, creative mind of Dellanna O'Brien. None of the ministries has been more successful than the nationally recognized Christian Women's Job Corps. She was also instrumental in the establishment of the WMU Foundation, which has enhanced WMU's financial base for service.

When, in 1998, Dellanna suffered a stroke, she weathered the challenges of that adversity with the same faith and valor she lent to her service at the helm of WMU. It was not until two years later that she retired, and even then, she merely moved to other avenues of service. She continues in overseas ministries and in sharing her passion for missions both in America and abroad.

Dellanna O'Brien has earned the respect of many people. On her tenth anniversary, the organization established the Dellanna West O'Brien Leadership Award, a fitting acknowledgement of the power of the legacy of her life and ministry. The two presidents who worked so closely with her recall her heart and passion for missions and for people. Wanda Lee praises her great warmth and sense of humor, her deep and genuine love for people. Carolyn Miller came to see her as always "the same committed Christian. No matter what the circumstances, her Christlike spirit never wavered. Dellanna O'Brien always conducted herself in a manner worthy of the gospel." One of Dellanna's daughters comments freely on her mother's strengths: "Perseverance is her hallmark. Mother is *always* gracious, no matter the circumstances around her. And wherever she is and whatever she is doing, Mother is still a servant."

Thousands of women remember and gain strength from one of Dellanna O'Brien's favorite maxims: God isn't finished with us yet.

supporting, praying for, giving to, and being involved in missions, as well as supporting the Cooperative Program and the Lottie Moon Christmas Offering and the Annie Armstrong Easter Offering.[31]

By 1993, SBC was deep in the midst of conflict. In an effort for control, those in positions of leadership made plans to restructure the SBC. Not surprisingly, WMU continued to come under scrutiny as SBC leadership proceeded to plan organizational changes.

In 1994, unknown to WMU, the Foreign Mission Board (FMB) applied for a trademark on the Lottie Moon Christmas Offering. Ten months later, WMU learned of the attempt. When confronted, the FMB said they were trying to prevent churches from using the Lottie Moon offering to raise funds for causes other than the FMB. As the action became public knowledge, the FMB received overwhelmingly negative response to what many Southern Baptists viewed as a surreptitious action. The Board consequently dropped its efforts to trademark the offering. Nevertheless, wheels had been set in motion,

Wanda Lee: President 1996–2000, Executive Director 2000–

Live the Call, Wanda Lee's first book, is synonymous with Wanda Lee herself. It is how she performed her role as WMU's seventh executive director. Wanda Lee was the only chief executive officer of Woman's Missionary Union who served first as national president, then as executive director.

Wanda Seay was born in Russellville, Alabama, but lived in south Florida until she was 16. She noted four distinct calls in her life: the call to salvation, the call to minister through nursing, the call to the missions field, and the call to become WMU's chief officer.

The very characteristics that made her a successful nurse for 30 years were traits and skills used by God to mold her into a keen and dynamic executive. She was process-oriented, skillful, organized, orderly, and brimming over with compassion and concern for the world at her door *and* far beyond America's borders. A discerning women's leader viewed Wanda in this position at this time in Baptist history, and observed: "How appropriate that God has placed you here at a point in time when we need healing."

Wanda credited three WMU women, all over age 50 and members of the first church that called her husband, Larry, as pastor, for taking a "greenhorn," first-time pastor's wife, loving her, and shaping her missions heart. The women introduced her to the prayer calendar, and her heart opened to the world. And for more than 20 years, Wanda Lee was involved in every level of WMU. She served as an Acteens leader for more than 25 years, and she participated in numerous missions trips at home and abroad as a nurse volunteer and member of BNF.

A full-time nurse, mother, and pastor's wife, Wanda worked in WMU, first locally and then in her association, and later as Georgia state president. In 1996, she was elected national president. Small wonder the women of national WMU looked to her for leadership.

Wanda's first 10 years of national service, as president and then executive director, were packed with challenges. Dellanna O'Brien's illness meant Wanda spent extra time at national headquarters helping steer the organization through a series of complex circumstances. The restructuring of the SBC presented a plethora of problems for WMU, not the least of which was the need to maintain relationships in order to fulfill their missions mandate.

Among the many facets of the job was the need to be a skillful public-relations officer. Wanda masterfully filled the role. She was gifted at guiding WMU through a time of transition, and her move from president to executive director meant seamless leadership at a vital juncture in Baptist history. Wanda Lee spent countless hours and covered thousands of miles, communicating the vision of our missions challenge.

Following Wanda's leadership, WMU began the new decade with the Blueprint for the 21st Century, a redefining of the vision for fulfilling the Great Commission. They took a new look at the missions education needs of the local church and developed a far-reaching presence on the World Wide Web.

Farsighted but practical. Tender but tough. Efficient but empathetic. Quiet but dynamic. Wanda Lee may be a study in contrasts. She was clearly a dynamic and dedicated woman of God, a sterling example of how God can impassion and inspire the service of a woman who lives the call.

and WMU felt compelled to place legal trademarks on the Lottie Moon Christmas Offering® and the Annie Armstrong Easter Offering®.

The SBC restructuring proposal passed at the 1995 SBC meeting. During the planning stages, the SBC again tried to persuade WMU to accept agency status. WMU's decision was to publicly affirm their desire to remain an auxiliary. Consequently, when the restructuring plans became public, WMU had been left out of the assignment for missions education as well as responsibility for the two missions offerings that WMU had initiated more than a century before. Under pressure, the Executive Committee of the SBC adopted a resolution of appreciation for the contributions of WMU. The resolution welcomed WMU's "continued voluntary contribution in mobilizing mission prayer support, and promotion of missions offerings stimulating the missionary spirit within the Convention."[32]

WMU continued with undiminished tenacity to remain true to its calling and focus. And the remarkable women of WMU, all the way to the grassroots level, remained steadfast in supporting missions.

Carolyn Miller, who served as president in the first half of the decade, saw as the biggest challenge keeping WMU focused on its central task in the midst of great conflict and uncertainty in the SBC. WMU leadership made every effort *not* to become distracted by the massive pressures mounted against the organization, but instead to concentrate on keeping WMU centered on its true mandate.[33]

Dellanna O'Brien appealed to the WMU constituency: "WMU is committed to raising high the flag of missions." She further urged that committed women and girls, as "laborers together with God, . . . continue to move forward with boldness and energy into our second century of missionary work."[34]

And, at the 1999 January Board Meeting, the Blueprint for the 21st Century recommendations were presented with a bold vision statement and nine core values. As their vision, the body adopted:

> WMU challenges Christian believers to understand and be radically involved in the mission of God.

The values center around prayer, upholding the priesthood of the believer, nurturing youth and adults in missions, developing missions leaders, and using personal gifts in responding to human needs and the Great Commission. (See the nine core values in the appendix.)

In March 2000, Wanda Lee became the seventh executive director of WMU, and in June 2000, Janet Hoffman of Louisiana was selected as national president. WMU entered a new century *and* a new millennium buffeted on every side by the stormy waves of controversies beyond their control. Nevertheless, they exhibited amazing resiliency and an extraordinary ability to focus on their goals. Undaunted, WMU entered a new millennium, never doubting the faithfulness of the One they served.

14
2001–2006

Only a small percentage of people throughout history have been able to welcome in a new millennium. The sense of history surrounding such a momentous point in time was viewed by the membership of Woman's Missionary Union as the ideal time to renew their changeless commitment to winning the world for Christ. They began the new millennium by electing Wanda Lee as WMU's seventh executive director. Lee, with her singular organizational and people skills, exhibited an unwavering faith in what God was going to do through the approximately 1 million members of this organization committed to fulfilling Christ's commission.

Wanda Lee had been national president since 1996, and the first year of the new century, Janet Hoffman of Louisiana stepped into that position. Lee and Hoffman had known one another for years and worked together on numerous projects. Now they forged a new team that proved extremely effective.

The first half of the first decade of the new millennium saw several never-before-imagined cataclysmic occurrences. The terrorist action on the morning of September 11, 2001, changed not only the US, but indeed our whole world forever. A tsunami hit Asia in 2004, and in 2005, the worst natural disaster in US history hit the nation in the form of hurricanes. WMU was quick to respond to meet the crying needs spawned by such havoc, as the organization experienced a new sense of urgency in sharing the message of hope in God with a fractured society.

Initiating Initiatives

During the first year of the new century, WMU selected as its tagline Discover the Joy of Missions[SM], encouraging women and churches to relish the sense of jubilation that results from missions involvement. Several promising new initiatives began in this new decade. Sisters Who Care, launched in June 2000, is a program to develop Women on Mission® organizations in Southern Baptist African American churches. The first national conference for Sisters Who Care was held at Ridgecrest in 2003, with over 300 enthusiastic women taking part.[1] The next national event was scheduled for September 2005, but Hurricane Katrina forced its postponement to February 2006.

Impact Northeast began early in 2000 when partnerships were formed between 11 state conventions—5 in the Northeast and 6 in the South. Leaders in the southern states partnered with leaders in the northeastern states to strengthen the work of Southern Baptists in this highest concentration of lostness in the US. National WMU was invited to the table along with WMU leadership and members from all 11 states. In 2005, one small Alabama team of seasoned WMU leaders worked for one week with the Baptist Convention of Pennsylvania-South Jersey, meeting with women and pastors who were excited about missions and saw the vision of what a missions organization in their churches could do. That one week produced 21 new missions organizations.[2]

International Initiatives was begun during this time as a response to the long-range planning project Blueprint for the 21st Century. Longtime Illinois state executive director Evelyn Tully helped national WMU develop a strategy for partnering with believers abroad in meeting needs directly pertaining to women. Tully looked at issues like poverty, health care, and sex trafficking. She led the new program to focus on three strategic 3-year partnerships with Greece, Croatia, and with missionaries in Paris. Since the program's inception, a new partnership has been forged with Moldova, focusing on missions education development and issues of sex trafficking. Actually, one approach involves both of these aims, as Moldovan-style GA® and Acteens® groups are being organized to provide a forum for dealing with this grave issue affecting Moldovan young women.

In 2004 International Initiatives sent three teams to share love and the message of God's hope at the 2004 Summer Olympics in Athens, Greece.[3] And in 2006, a team was sent to Italy for the Winter Games.

The new century has seen the emergence of several new missions outreach initiatives. MissionsFEST℠ and FamilyFEST℠ enable volunteers from age six and up to be involved in ministries such as sports camps to construction, Bible clubs, health fairs, and even block parties and landscaping. By 2005, nearly 1,100 volunteers worked in five different locations, stretching from New York City to Tijuana, Mexico.[4]

Technology was an important consideration when establishing the new headquarters building in the 1980s, and WMU continues to make great technological strides into the new millennium. In 2001, MissionSmart was launched[5] and an Internet strategy project was approved the same year. The Web site www.missionsmart.net provides a user-friendly resource for making missions plans successful, whether for an individual or a church.

In 2004, a new program design for collegiate women in missions was approved, based on a Web site for college women (www.missionsinterchange.com).

WMU's presence on the World Wide Web grows daily in the new century with Web sites in service and a robust, newly redesigned online store, www.wmustore.com.

A high moment came in 2003 with the visit of Sook Jae Lee, executive director of Korea Woman's Missionary Union. Sook Jae Lee and her team were preparing for the 50th anniversary celebration of WMU in Korea, to be held in 2004. During her historic visit, WMU leaders of the two nations had a unique opportunity to share ideas and plans for the future.[6] In return, Wanda Lee and Janet Hoffman visited the Korea WMU offices, honoring their 50 years with a gift of $5,000 to the newly formed endowment through the WMU Foundation on behalf of the Baptist World Alliance Women's Department.

A New Look in Materials

Seeking to meet the changing needs of local, associational, and statewide organizations, WMU introduced WMU How-Tos in 2002, replacing the WMU guides of the 1990s. The next year, a new GA Motto, GA Pledge, and GA Scripture Verse were approved; and Acteens resources were updated with *Acteens Leader* and *The Mag,* which replaced *Accent.*

In 2004, Hispanic audiences noticed an update to their missions magazine, *Nuestra Tarea;* and missions leaders received an updated resource, *Missions Leader*[SM], which replaced *Dimension.*

Even the headquarters building was updated when in 2005 a gift shop was opened in the lobby as a part of the Weatherford Parlor, allowing visitors and staff the opportunity to view and purchase WMU®, New Hope®, and WorldCrafts[SM] items during building hours.

New Hope Publishers, a WMU imprint, continues to grow in the new century. Distribution in secular bookstores allows an ever-wider audience to be touched by the message of hope through those unique Christian books. It has expanded to publish books in three lines: a line for women and families; a missional line; and a line for Bible studies and teaching resources.[7]

Successful Programs Plus New Approaches

Project HELP continued with the first 2-year emphasis of the new century on Literacy. Women across the country were energized to share the gift of reading with thousands of people who had never had the opportunity to learn.

Restorative Justice was the emphasis for 2002 and 2003. Entire congregations became involved in bring healing and wholeness to victims, offenders, and law enforcement professional affected by crime. The subsequent Project HELP aimed at poverty became the first 4-year emphasis. As a result, WMU started a variety of ongoing programs to address poverty and provide families with avenues for hands-on missions. Ideas and resources in print and online are available to guide compassionate women and whole churches into life-changing ministries.[8]

For more than 20 years, WMU has sponsored Baptist Nursing Fellowship℠ (BNF®), a part of Baptist Medical Dental Fellowship. As a professional health-care organization, BNF engages health-care professionals in voluntary mission service in America and overseas. It provides life-changing experience, both for the nurses serving *and* the recipients of their ministries. In 2006 there were at least 1,000 nursing professionals giving volunteer service through BNF groups in 29 states.

The Missionary Housing Office, begun in the 1990s, continues to touch the lives of many international missionaries on stateside assignment each year. In 2005 alone, 539 individuals, churches, and associations provided 587 houses across the country for international missionaries back in the States. This peace of mind offered to God's servants needing a home away from home is an invaluable encouragement to these missionary partners in service.

Through the Missionary Housing Office, WMU has partnered with hundreds of missionaries like Jan and Mark Moses, missionaries to the Philippines. Compassionate

Baptists in the Dallas/Fort Worth area and WMU joined forces to provide emergency housing for the Moseses and their five children. Both Jan and Mark were diagnosed with cancer and needed immediate medical care and a place to live. A place was quickly provided, helping to meet a crucial need for a family pushed to the limit. They are one family among hundreds who have received a helping hand when they most needed it.

Training Leaders, Leading in Ministries

Training Effective Leaders (TEL), which began in the 1990s, has become instrumental in preparing women for strategic ministries in the new millennium. At first, one TEL conference was held each year, but by 2003, two sessions a year in different parts of the country have become a regular feature of the training series.

The Mississippi River Ministry (MRM) is a partnership between seven states that border the lower Mississippi River, the North American Mission Board (NAMB), and WMU. It touches lives of people like Ruth Turner. The 81-year-old's life was forever changed when a group of youth volunteered to help. Ruth's house desperately needed painting, but she could not afford to buy the paint. So the youth team spent a week painting her house. Months later, when Ruth became gravely ill with cancer, she had not listened to neighbors who tried to tell her about Jesus. But she *would* listen to the pastor who had brought the youth group to help her. Yes, God used a paintbrush and the MRM to change Ruth Turner's life.[9]

One successful ministry leads to another. Following the continued success of MRM, the Appalachian Regional Ministry (ARM) , involving part of ten states, was started. State conventions, NAMB, and WMU work together on this project to answer massive requests. Meeting human and spiritual needs alike are the heart of the ministry.

More than 19 million people live in these areas of need. Parts of Appalachia are 80 to 90 percent unchurched.[10]

Bessie McPeak is a shining example of creative ministry in the Appalachian region. She demonstrates God's love with a diaper bag. She meets needs of young mothers by providing diapers, baby clothes, and God's message of hope. Having grown up in coal mining country in Kentucky, Bessie understands poverty firsthand. She declares: "Nobody *chooses* to be poor. It's because of lack of education and jobs."

In 2003, Bessie's resources ran out; but after pleading with God for direction, an opportunity came for radio and TV interviews. Word of Bessie's diaper bag ministry spread and help flooded in: diapers, clothes, food, volunteers, and still they came. And Bessie and her husband pass on the message of love and hope from a diaper bag that miraculously stays full.[11]

Borderland Ministry follows in the tradition of MRM and ARM. This new project is a network of states, WMU, NAMB, International Mission Board (IMB), LifeWay, and the Mexico Baptist Convention. The network exists to communicate ministry opportunities and coordinate efforts along the US southwest border and in Mexico. It evolved as WMU Volunteer Connection® was preparing for MissionsFEST in San Diego and Tijuana, Mexico. It promises to be an ongoing partnership with individuals and churches working in these areas.[12]

An extremely successful project was in place at a strategic time to meet a desperate need. WMU has been sponsoring Pure Water, Pure Love℠ since 1997 when the program was transferred to WMU from the Brotherhood Commission. The program has been around helping provide safe water for missionaries since 1995. Within days of the horrific tsunami which hit Southeast Asia in December 2004, WMU sent $37,000 worth of water purification equipment to Indonesia to help save lives. In 2005, Pure Water, Pure Love provided the first pure water system in an area of Tijuana, Mexico, where refugees were living in squalor without an adequate water supply. Partnering with a NAMB missionary and director of missions, a Mexican Baptist pastor, and others, water is now available to thousands for free with a testimony of living water as well through truth in Christ.

WMU also stood ready to help when Hurricane Katrina devastated the US southern coast in 2005. A disaster response team formed quickly, and national WMU established contact with the leadership in the affected states and kept a pulse on the influx of evacuees in all areas of the country and how best to help everyone involved. Knowing that Southern Baptist Disaster Relief was up and running in so many areas, national WMU's Volunteer Connection® turned their focus on a local ministry in Birmingham, CareNET. A HEART Fund grant was able to assist this ministry through the Birmingham Baptist Association to continue helping the hundreds who had come to the area needing a place to live.

Prior to Katrina, Volunteer Connection was beginning to launch On Call Missions Teams, groups of people who could mobilize within a short period of time. Some of the first teams served in Metairie, Louisiana, just a few weeks after Katrina hit. Many residents were still not back in the area, but there were those who needed assistance with food, hygiene, household goods, cleaning, and much more. Several individuals and teams continued their volunteer work through the rebuilding process.

WorldCrafts Helping the World

The WorldCrafts℠ ministry builds upon success, as women and men receive new heart when they are able to support their families and eternal hope, as more and more of them have opportunities to learn about Christ and His gift of redemption. By 2005, WorldCrafts had expanded to 31 countries and more than 300 different items.[13]

On the edge of a major Indonesian city live thousands of squatters, some in an unused portion of a graveyard. One woman earned pennies a day rolling cigarettes, and another woman and her children were abandoned by her husband. These women with little or no income whatsoever met a worker who taught them how to make puppets, and how much God loves them. Now 8 women meet each week to sew together and hear stories about God. In Madagascar, 25 women, all the only bread-winners for their families, embroider for WorldCrafts, and receive classes in health and nutrition and a chance to hear the gospel.[14]

Christian Women's Job Corps on the Move

One of WMU's most exciting ministries, Christian Women's Job Corps® (CWJC®), has gone from one success to another as it dramatically impacts women and their entire families. The number of CWJC sites in 2005 increased 30 percent from the year before. Christian Men's Job Corps[SM] (CMJC[SM]) locations were developing as well. In all, 127 sites around the US were helping countless women and men gain self-confidence and a purpose in life as they find hope in Christ. In 2006, some CWJC locations are expanding to provide not just job training but actual jobs.

Success stories abound. Melissa is one of thousands. She came to CWJC in 2002, having just endured divorce after 14 years of marriage and three children. Married at age 15, she only had an eighth-grade education, and had never held a public job. Melissa was overwhelmed, distraught, and engulfed by hopelessness. Then she heard about CWJC. After her 15-week course, Melissa beamed: "The best thing I have learned is that I am deeply loved and completely forgiven." The week of graduation from CWJC, Melissa also attended another graduation—to receive her GED diploma. Two years later she had a degree as a nursing assistant and a full-time job. The radiant young mother is happily serving as an encourager to new CWJC young women. Multiply Melissa's story a thousand times and the value of such a program becomes increasingly apparent.[15]

Understanding the Umbrella

These new and continually expanding ministries and projects of Woman's Missionary Union illustrate a new phenomenon—the *expanding* umbrella of WMU. Its scope continues to extend beyond women, youth, and children. The WMU umbrella is large enough to include the entire local church in its missions heart and involvement. As WMU provides materials and initiatives that inspire all Baptists to be involved in missions outreach, it becomes a premier resource for the local church. Gone is the old view of WMU being limited to a group of women praying, serving, and giving. Women on Mission is just *one* of the groups under the missions umbrella. There are Mission Friends, Missions Interchange, GA, Acteens, Children in Action, Youth on Mission[SM], and Adults on Mission[SM]. Plus, in 2007, Families on Missions will be added.[16] The WMU umbrella has expanded to include all people who wish to serve.

WMU and Missions Giving

Statistics illustrate the effectiveness of the WMU umbrella. A 2003 study shows WMU's influence on the local church and on the cause of missions advance. More than 40,000 Baptist churches participated in a survey about missions giving. Approximately half of the churches had WMU involvement and the other half did not. The results were telling.

In churches with WMU organizations, Cooperative Program giving was more than three times as great. The disparity was greater when comparing giving to the Lottie Moon Christmas Offering[®] (LMCO[SM]) and the Annie

Armstrong Easter Offering® (AAEO^SM). Churches with WMU organizations gave more than four times as much to the two missions offerings. The LMCO shows the impact WMU organizations have on giving. In "WMU" churches, the total LMCO in 2003 was $80,934,767. In those churches with no WMU, the total was $21,773,232. The average missions gifts per member for churches with no WMU was $46.32. Churches *with* WMU, on the other hand, gave $103.70 per member.

The Thriving Foundation

In order to ensure continued worldwide outreach, WMU maintains emphases on the funds that make such strategic work possible. Elected president of the WMU Foundation in 2001, David George brought strong managerial and people skills to the post. The Foundation continues to grow and flourish each year. Because people across the nation give generously, exciting opportunities to share the good news increase.

The Foundation is set apart from similar entities, for this one attracts donors who give their hearts, prayers, and lives to support missions. Several projects fall under the direction of the Foundation. The Vision Fund supports all WMU ministries, and the Humanitarian Emergency Aid for Rebuilding Tomorrow (HEART) Fund reaches out to emergency needs worldwide, providing "heart" for them in the form of monetary hope. The Second Century Fund also falls under Foundation supervision and continues to grow each year as it provides resources for women's leadership development around the world.[17]

The new century saw a shift in Southern Baptist Convention's (SBC) relationship with Baptists worldwide through the Baptist World Alliance (BWA). This shift necessitated a response from WMU as to their cooperative ministry with Baptist women of all nations. In February 2004, the SBC Executive Committee recommended withdrawing from the BWA, and messengers at the June SBC annual meeting passed the recommendation.

The Executive Board of WMU, meeting in January of that year, discussed at length their long history of cooperative effort with the women of the BWA, and the historical background of WMU's involvement. WMU had been a leading force in the founding of the Women's Department of BWA, itself an auxiliary to BWA. In a significant 100 percent vote, the Executive Board resolved:

That Woman's Missionary Union affirm our historic relationship with the Women's Department of the Baptist World Alliance and the North American Baptist Women's Union, and that we commit to continue promoting and participating in the Baptist Women's World Day of Prayer and offering.[18]

At the February meeting of the SBC Executive Committee, WMU president Janet Hoffman voiced WMU's affirmation of the women's department of BWA. She appealed to the committee that the SBC seek reconciliation with the BWA rather than separation. She reported that WMU stood unanimously in voting to affirm their "relationship with BWA. It was as if they stood as one," she said, in expressing WMU's love for and continuing partnership with the Christian women of other lands.[19]

As a result, Baptist women worldwide have responded with gratitude and joy at WMU's supportive stance, as cooperative efforts to reach the world for Christ go forward in unity.

Forging the Future

The Vision 2010 Task Force was appointed by Janet Hoffman in 2004 to lay out broad directions for the future of WMU's work. For 117 years, WMU has maintained a single focus—missions. Its purpose is to equip preschoolers, children, youth, and adults so they might understand and find their unique place in radical missions involvement. The vast majority of people who partner with WMU are members of Southern Baptist churches. That has always been the case. WMU resources those churches and any others who desire to engage in missions through the resources and opportunities afforded by WMU. The privilege of rallying support for Southern Baptist missionaries is not one that WMU takes lightly, as members and leaders pray daily for missionaries and their needs, and call on the church to give sacrificially so the men and women on the field may continue serving. Along with this responsibility, WMU strives to continue encouraging people God is calling to serve as missionaries and volunteers.

Facing challenges is nothing new to the intrepid women of the new millennium's WMU. They are women who do not know how to fail. The passion for passing on the vision that stirred the hearts of their pioneer mothers has not diminished in the 200-plus years since Polly Webb organized those missions-hearted women in Boston. The immediacy of the Great Commission remains changeless in their vision of the task lying ahead.

Because of an uncertain world climate of unrest and turmoil, the future of any organization is often questioned. Frequently, national and state WMU leaders and thousands of faithful WMU women in local churches across the country are asked, "In light of all that is going on, what is the future of Woman's Missionary Union?" The question might best be answered by taking a look at the very beginning of Baptist missions in America. In 1812, Ann and Adoniram Judson sailed for Burma as America's first missionaries. They became Baptists by conviction while on the high seas, and became the catalysts for Baptist churches in America to forge a denomination in order to support the Judsons.[20]

Adoniram Judson came to stand alone in missions history, both for what God did through his commitment

Janet Hoffman: 2000–2005

 "God is calling you, Janet. Listen." One of Janet Hoffman's most cherished memories is of hearing her grandfather say those words. That challenge uttered in his gentle voice has never left her heart.

Janet Thompson, born in Tulsa, Oklahoma, in 1935, had a wonderful mother who mentored her in missions and was a treasure of a pastor's wife who was "what I thought a pastor's wife ought to be!" Her childhood hero, however, was her grandfather, Charles F. Siler, a Missouri Baptist preacher. With a heart that encompassed the world, his influence was profound.

Janet was a Sunbeam at age 3. She spent summers with her Missouri grandparents where she met her first missionary. And she heard her first missionary speaker at Falls Creek (Oklahoma's state Baptist assembly). As an early teen, Janet led Sunbeams, and by 14, she taught Mission Vacation Bible Schools.

Moving to Houston as a teenager, she graduated from Baylor University, but not before meeting Harvey Hoffman, a young ministerial student. Following graduation they married, and it wasn't long until Janet Hoffman was a pastor's wife. Deeply involved in WMU, she held numerous leadership positions in Texas and Louisiana and especially relished working with GAs. A high school teacher, and mother of three, Janet didn't know the meaning of "free time." She considered her foremost commitment to nurture their children, and she mentored them in a missions lifestyle.

Janet was president of Louisiana WMU from 1991 to 1995 and national recording secretary from 1996 to 2000. She followed Wanda Lee in 2000 as national president, the same year Wanda was elected executive director. Of like commitment and call, their leadership was strong and effective.

The missions passion planted deeply in the heart of the little girl from Oklahoma continued to flow outward in ever-expanding circles of influence. Known for her gracious spirit and unassuming demeanor, Janet was a leader with a core of great strength fired by a spirit of deep faith and that ever-present passion for missions.

Janet Hoffman faced diverse situations that called forth the best in her. At every opportunity, she emphasized: "Missions. That's our middle name." Janet recognized the need to cultivate relationships with other Baptist entities; and always in her work, both with the women of WMU and with the SBC, she reinforced WMU's singular focus on missions.

Janet Hoffman will be remembered for her courageous stand for the women of the Baptist World Alliance. In 2004, she addressed the SBC Executive Committee and championed the Baptist women of the world, expressing WMU's determination to continue serving alongside them.

Janet worked tirelessly on WMU's plan for the future—Vision 2010—and found time to use another of her talents, writing. For more than 20 years, she wrote curriculum for WMU and a missionary biography for youth, *The Pattersons: Missionary Publishers*. While president, she wrote two books, *God Is Calling You: And Other Things My Granddad Taught Me*, and *ChristLight: Reflecting the Image of Christ in the Real World*.

Janet Hoffman left her gracious stamp on the character of Woman's Missionary Union. Her son Jess says, "Her life, summed up in one word, is *sacrifice*. She sacrificed her time, energy, and money to give to missions offerings and mission service. Her passion for missions is the fabric of her life."

and as a symbol of the power of the Word of God to change lives forever. In the last years of his extraordinary ministry, Judson was frequently asked: "What do you see for the future of missions?" His answer was invariably the same—an answer from one who had been through the refiner's fire: "The future is as bright as the promises of God."

Even after 150 years, that historic affirmation is still embraced by Woman's Missionary Union. Question: How do you see the future of Woman's Missionary Union? Answer: The future is as bright as the promises of God.

Kaye Miller: 2005–

Kaye Willis Miller, the 18th national president of Woman's Missionary Union, marks another WMU "first." She is the first MK (missionary kid) to lead WMU. Growing up more Thai than American, she is uniquely a third-culture woman, and appropriately a world citizen, with a burning passion for the world to know Christ.

Kaye Willis was born in the US, but was only in kindergarten when her parents were appointed as medical missionaries to Thailand. Her mother and father were without question the greatest influences on her life. She saw each day the intensity of their service, the passion of their commitment, the urgency they felt as they shared in word and action the message of hope in Christ. She watched her mother nurture women in the villages and saw her father exemplifying Christ's compassion as he ministered daily to patients at the Baptist hospital in Bangkla.

No one spot impacted her life more than the leprosy clinic where her father shared the story of salvation and operated on twisted and useless hands maimed by that dread disease. One day, as Kaye watched her dad minister to a leper, she saw him cradle gnarled and disfigured fingers in his gentle surgeon's hands and explain to the patient how she could obtain eternal joy and healing. As Kaye listened to the gospel in the Thai language, God spoke to *her* heart, and she trusted Him right there. Forever imprinted in her mind is the image of healing hands and the assurance that the Great Physician had touched and forever healed her heart.

WMU had a profound effect on young Kaye, growing up in a completely different culture. She was a GA and an Acteen in faraway Thailand, going all the way to Queen Regent in Service. Kaye entered Baylor University in 1972. America "on her own" was a shock, but each step of the way God provided every need: friends; a job; a family (former international missionaries) who took Kaye into their hearts; and even a familiar roommate, a girl she had met in fifth grade while on stateside assignment.

She graduated with a degree in nursing, and while working at Baylor Hospital, she met Mark Miller on a blind date. They married a year later and moved to Pine Bluff, Arkansas. More than two decades and four children later, Kaye considers her greatest accomplishment being a wife and mother (and now a grandmother as well). She expresses pure joy in seeing each child committed to Christ and His leadership.

WMU became a big part of Kaye's life and service. In her church she was GA director for nearly 20 years, then she "graduated" to Acteens director and director of Youth on Mission. Kaye Miller stepped into state leadership in 2002 when she was elected president of Arkansas WMU. Then in 2005, Janet Hoffman, another Baylor graduate, passed the gavel of the national presidency to Kaye.

Kaye sees tremendous challenges *and* opportunities ahead for WMU in the new millennium. She feels a sense of urgency—learned from her parents—to reach people with the news of hope. One of her goals is to guide state and national leaders in working together as a family in seeking the most productive ways to fulfill the Great Commission.

Mark Miller says his wife "has a unique ability to bring people together." She uses that gift along with her skills of organization and administration developed through years of work as a nurse as she shares a healing touch in service to WMU.

Notes

Chapter 1

[1]Timothy George, *Faithful Witness: The Life and Mission of William Carey* (Birmingham, AL: New Hope, 1991), 67–69.

[2]Paul Peas, *William Carey* (Leominster, England: Day One Publications, 2005), 56–68.

[3]Rosalie Hall Hunt, *Bless God and Take Courage: The Judson History and Legacy* (Valley Forge: Judson Press, 2005), viii.

[4]Ibid., 62.

[5]Bill Leonard, *Baptist Ways: A History* (Valley Forge: Judson Press, 2003), 214–15.

[6]Robert G. Torbet, *Venture of Faith* (Valley Forge: Judson Press, 1955), 190.

[7]Catherine B. Allen, *Laborers Together with God* (Birmingham, AL: Woman's Missionary Union, 1987*)*, 228–29.

[8]Ibid., 228.

[9]Allen, *Laborers Together with God*, 228–29. Note: Graves was mentor to Martha McIntosh, who became the first president of WMU. McIntosh later wrote of Graves: "It would be impossible in writing a history of woman's mission work in the South to omit Mrs. Ann J. Graves, the originator and moving spirit of the work."

[10]Catherine B. Allen, *The New Lottie Moon Story* (Nashville: Broadman Press, 1980), 67–68, 110–13.

Chapter 2

[1]*Baptist Argus*, March 16, 1898; *Texas Baptist—Extra*, May 12, 1883.

[2]Ibid.
[3]Ibid.

Chapter 3

[1]Susan Taylor Pollard, "Enlistment of State Forces and Organization of Woman's Missionary Union," Early Leaflet Collection, WMU Archives.
[2]Marjean Patterson, *Covered Foundations: A History of Mississippi Woman's Missionary Union* (Jackson: Mississippi Woman's Missionary Union, 1978), 14.
[3]WMU Annual Report, 1892 and 1895; Executive Committee Minutes, WMU, SBC, June 9 and September 2, 1892; *Washington Post*, May 12, 1895; Armstrong to Frost, January 26, 1897; SBC Annual 1986, HMB Report.

Chapter 4

[1]Simmons to T. T. Eaton, W. W. Landrum, and E. Y. Mullins, November 22, 1901.
[2]Una Roberts Lawrence, *Winning the Border: Baptist Missions Among the Spanish-Speaking Peoples of the Border* (Atlanta: Home Mission Board, SBC, 1935).
[3]WMU Annual Report 1909.

Chapter 5

[1]Executive Committee, WMU, SBC, Policy, 1910–11.
[2]Note: Although contributions dropped during the Depression, WMU cut salaries and was able to keep Woman's Missionary Union Training School debt free. The Good Will Center in Louisville was sold in 1967, with funds later designated for the Second Century Fund for WMU leadership development.
[3]Note: By 1924, WMU reported total attendance at good will centers at 103,000. The number of WMU societies with operating centers grew to a high of 993 in 1935. To ensure adequate funding, WMU eventually gave them to the Home Mission Board.

[4]Note: By 1938, WMU was conducting approximately one-fourth of Southern Baptists' VBS efforts. They continued to promote Mission VBS until the 1950s when they turned the project over to the Sunday School Board.
[5]Note: Exceptions came in 1929 as Arizona affiliated and then in the 1940s when California WMU declared affiliation.

Chapter 6

[1]James F. Love, *Missionary Messages* (New York: George H. Doran Co., 1922).
[2]Note: *World Comrades* was followed by *Ambassador Life* for boys in 1946 and *Sunbeam Activities* and *Tell* by 1953.
[3]Executive Committee Minutes, WMU, SBC, June 3, 1925.

Chapter 8

[1]Catherine B. Allen, *A Century to Celebrate* (Birmingham, AL: Woman's Missionary Union, 1987), 158.
[2]Ibid, 351–52.
[3]Ibid., 72, 77. Note: When Hawaii achieved statehood in 1959, the FMB transferred its interests. Alaska joined WMU in the same way.
[4]Ibid., 226.
[5]Note: Hunt too continued the tradition of financial sacrifice for WMU professions. In coming to national WMU, Hunt took a cut in pay. In the many years to follow, she herself was paid only a few dollars more than her associates.
[6]Catherine Allen, *Laborers Together with God* (Birmingham, AL: Woman's Missionary Union, 1987), 203.

Chapter 10

[1]T. B. Maston in *Home Missions* magazine, September 1966.
[2]A few years after its formation, BYW was reorganized to include women aged 18 through 34. BYW extended to college campuses in 1977 and the United States Military Academy at West Point established a BYW in the 1980s.

Chapter 11
[1]Catherine B. Allen, *A Century to Celebrate* (Birmingham, AL: Woman's Missionary Union, 1987), 341.
[2]Ibid., 342–43.
[3]Ibid., 179.
[4]Sider's book has been updated twice since the 1970s.
[5]Allen, *A Century to Celebrate*, 163–64.

Chapter 12
[1]WMU Annual Report 1979, 3–4.
[2]WMU Annual Report 1980, 18.
[3]WMU Annual Report 1989, 17–18.
[4]WMU Annual Report 1985, 33.
[5]WMU Annual Report 1986, 43.
[6]WMU Annual Report 1986, 21–22.
[7]*Nuestra Tarea*, February 1993. Note: Doris Diaz retired in 1992 and died of cancer just a few months later.
[8]WMU Annual Report 1988, 25–26.
[9]WMU Annual Report 1985, 34.
[10]WMU Annual Report 1989, 39–41.
[11]WMU Minutes 1990.
[12]WMU Annual Report 1990, 43.
[13]WMU Annual Report 1984, 33.
[14]WMU Annual Report 1985, 35.
[15]WMU Annual Report 1989, 49.
[16]Interview with Christine Gregory, January 2006.
[17]By January 2006, over $1.2 million in grants had been awarded through the Second Century Fund.
[18]WMU Annual Report 1985, 38.
[19]WMU Annual Report 1990, 44.
[20]E. Luther Copeland, *The Southern Baptist Convention and the Judgment of History* (Lanham, MD: University Press of America, 1995), 98–99.
[21]Baptist Press release, March 6, 1995. Note: In 1995, the SBC Restructuring Committee formally asked that WMU become as agency; however, the desire of WMU's national

board was patently clear and WMU continued as *auxiliary.*
[22]WMU Annual Report 1988, 23.
[23]Interview with Carolyn Weatherford Crumpler, 2005.
[24]WMU Annual Report 1989, 25–26, 40–41.

Chapter 13
[1]WMU Annual Report 1992, 8; interview with Dellanna O'Brien, 2005.
[2]WMU Annual Report 1991, 9.
[3]WMU Annual Report 1992, 2.
[4]WMU Annual Report 1993, 2.
[5]WMU Annual Report 1992, 13.
[6]WMU Annual Report 1993, 14.
[7]WMU Annual Report 1992, 21–22.
[8]WMU Annual Report 1995. Note: *Royal Service* had actually been redesigned in October 1993, but further changes were considered needed.
[9]WMU Annual Report 1992, 20. Note: Missions Adventures was an individual achievement plan for Girls in Action. WMU Annual Report 1997.
[10]WMU Annual Report 1997, 18.
[11]WMU Annual Report 1998, 15.
[12]WMU Annual Report 1993, 10.
[13]WMU Annual Report 1997.
[14]WMU Annual Report 1995.
[15]WMU Annual Report 1996.
[16]WMU Annual Report 1998, 11.
[17]WMU Annual Report 2000, 10.
[18]WMU Annual Report 1999, 5.
[19]WMU Annual Report 1997, 8.
[20]WMU Annual Report 1999, 7.
[21]WMU Annual Report 2002, 15.
[22]Trudy Johnson, WMJ Report, April 2002.
[23]WMU Annual Report 1994, 6.
[24]WMU Annual Report 1995, 5.

[25]WMU Annual Report 1996, 10.
[26]WMU Annual Report 1998, 13.
[27]WMU Annual Report 2000, 3.
[28]WMU Annual Report 1999, 17–18.
[29]WMU Annual Report 1993, 8.
[30]Interview with Dellanna O'Brien, 2005
[31]WMU statement to SBC Executive Board in session in Richmond, Virginia, September 22, 1990.
[32]Sally Holt, "The SBC and the WMU: Issues of Power and Authority Relating to Organization and Structure" (dissertation, Vanderbilt University, May 2001), 78–80.
[33]Interview with Carolyn Miller, January 2006.
[34]Dellanna O'Brien, WMU Annual Report 1993, 3.

Chapter 14
[1]WMU Annual Report 2003, 10.
[2]Interview with Pat Ingram, Alabama WMU MEV leader, February 2006.
[3]WMU Annual Report 2004, 14.
[4]WMU Annual Report 2005, 16–17.
[5]WMU Annual Report 2001, 5.
[6]WMU Annual Report 2003, 23.
[7]WMU Annual Report 2005, 22–23.
[8]Interview with Jean Cullen, February 7, 2006.
[9]Sandy Wisdom-Martin, Gail Pietsrup, East St. Louis, MS, March 21, 2005.
[10]Appalachian Regional Ministry, www.arministry.org, 2005.
[11]Shirley Cox, "God's Love from a Diaper Bag," *Missions Mosaic*, October 2004, 8–11.
[12]WMU Annual Report 2005, 11.
[13]WMU Annual Report 2005, 19.
[14]WorldCrafts Catalog 2004–2005, 8, 25.
[15]Interview with Linda Henry, Alabama CWJC coordinator, February 2006.

[16]Note: Projects such as FamilyFEST and MissionsFEST involve men, women, children, and youth.
[17]WMU Annual Report 2005, 24.
[18]General Session of WMU Executive Board, January 12, 2004.
[19]Art Toalston, "BWA Withdrawal Recommendation Approved for Vote by SBC Messengers in Indianapolis," Baptist Press, February 17, 2004.
[20]Rosalie Hall Hunt, *Bless God and Take Courage: The Judson History and Legacy* (Valley Forge: Judson Press, 2005).

Appendix

Presidents

1888–1892	Martha E. McIntosh (later Mrs. Theodore Percy Bell)
1892–1894	Fannie Exile Scudder Heck
1894–1895	Abby Manly Gwathmey (Mrs. William Henry)
1895–1899	Fannie Exile Scudder Heck
1899–1903	Sarah Jessie Davis Stakely (Mrs. Charles A.)
1903–1906	Lillie Easterby Barker (Mrs. John A.)
1906–1915	Fannie Exile Scudder Heck
1916–1925	Minnie Lou Kennedy James (Mrs. W. C.)
1925–1933	Ethlene Boone Cox (Mrs. W. J.)
1933–1945	Laura Dell Malotte Armstrong (Mrs. F. W.)
1945–1956	Olive Brinson Martin (Mrs. George R.)
1956–1963	Marie Wiley Mathis (Mrs. R. L.)
1963–1969	Helen Long Fling (Mrs. Robert)
1969–1975	Marie Wiley Mathis (Mrs. R. L.)
1975–1981	Christine Burton Gregory (Mrs. A. Harrison)
1981–1986	Dorothy Elliott Sample (Mrs. Richard H.)
1986–1991	Marjorie Jones McCullough (Mrs. Glendon)
1991–1996	Carolyn Miller (Mrs. Jack)
1996–2000	Wanda S. Lee (Mrs. Larry)
2000–2005	Janet T. Hoffman (Mrs. Harvey)
2005–	Kaye Miller (Mrs. Mark)

Executive Directors

(Corresponding Secretary was title until 1937; Executive Secretary 1937–1975; Executive Director after 1975.)

1888–1906	Annie Walker Armstrong
1907–1912	Edith Campbell Crane (later Mrs. Samuel T. Lanham)
1912–1948	Kathleen Moore Mallory
1948–1974	Alma Hunt

1974–1989	Carolyn Weatherford (later Mrs. Joseph Crumpler)
1989–1999	Dellanna West O'Brien (Mrs. Bill)
2000–	Wanda S. Lee (Mrs. Larry)

WMU Core Values

• We uphold the foundational principles of the priesthood of every believer and the autonomy and uniqueness of each local church in carrying out the Great Commission.

• We embrace the strategic role of prayer and giving for missionaries and missions needs.

• We recognize the role of family in discipleship and missions development.

• We recognize the giftedness of women and girls and accept the responsibility to help them use their gifts in serving Christ.

• We accept the responsibility for nurturing preschoolers, children, youth, and adults in missions.

• We accept the responsibility for developing and equipping missions leaders.

• We accept the biblical mandate to respond to human need with actions modeled by Jesus Christ and with the message of God's redemptive plan.

• We partner with other Great Commission Christians to lead a lost world to Christ.

• We believe that Jesus Christ, Son of God, gave His life a sacrifice for the salvation of all the people of the world, fulfilling God's plan for the ages as revealed in the Bible, God's Holy Word.

The Woman's Hymn
Tune: "Come, Thou Almighty King" (music by Felice de Giardini, 1716–1976)
Written by Fannie E. S. Heck
Printed in WMU Year Book 1913–14

Come, women, wide proclaim
Life through your Savior slain;
Sing evermore.
Christ, God's effulgence bright,
Christ, who arose in might,
Christ, who crowns you with light,
Praise and adore.

Come, clasping children's hands,
Sisters from many lands
Teach to adore.
For the sin-sick and worn,
The weak and over-borne,
All who in darkness mourn,
Pray, work, yet more.

Work with your courage high,
Sing of the daybreak nigh,
Your love outpour.
Stars shall your brow adorn,
Your heart leap with the morn
And, by His love up-borne,
Hope and adore.

Then when the garnered field
Shall to our Master yield
A bounteous store.

Christ, hope of all the meek,
Christ, whom all earth shall seek,
Christ, your reward shall speak,
Joy evermore.

Timeline

1800
Mary "Polly" Webb organized women in Boston's Second Baptist Church to pray for missions.

1868
Ann Baker Graves invited women attending SBC meeting in Baltimore to meet for prayer concerning missions.

1871
Baptist women in Baltimore organized as Woman's Mission to Woman.

1887
Maryland Baptist women opened the Mission Rooms, from which missions literature was published and distributed.

1888
WMU organized as the Executive Committee of the Woman's Mission Societies (Auxiliary to Southern Baptist Convention) with Annie Armstrong becoming first corresponding secretary.

Foreign missions offering established to send a missionary to China to relieve Lottie Moon.

1890
Name changed to Woman's Missionary Union, Auxiliary to Southern Baptist Convention.

WMU agreed to raise enough money to support all women foreign missionaries.

1892
First week of prayer held in connection with the Christmas offering.

1894
WMU began promoting work of Sunday School Board.

Extra offering to pay Foreign Mission Board debt exceeded goal.

1895
First week of prayer and offering to pay off Home Mission Board debt established.

1896
WMU adopted Sunbeam work at the request of the Foreign Mission Board.

1899
WMU recommended that the churches adopt a graded system of missionary education with organizations for all age levels, beginning with Baby Bands.

1900
WMU set up and funded the Home Mission Board's Church Building Loan Fund.

First WMU-sponsored churchwide event—a stewardship emphasis.

WMU opened the Margaret Home for children of missionaries who were overseas.

1906
WMU adopted a week of prayer for state missions.

WMU issued its first periodical, *Our Mission Fields.*

1907
WMU Training School started to train women missionaries.

Young Woman's Auxiliary became an official organization for women aged 16 through 25.

1908
The Calendar of Prayer adopted.

Order of Royal Ambassadors became the official name for missionary societies for boys.

1909
WMU purchased its first headquarters building in Baltimore, Maryland.

1910
Forerunner of mission action became a regular department of WMU work.

WMU chose its first annual watchword.
1912
WMU published its first Year Book.

1913
WMU recommended that larger societies be divided into circles.

WMU's first book-length history, *In Royal Service*, was published.

1914
Royal Service replaced *Our Mission Fields.*

Business Women's Circles began.

The name Girls' Auxiliary was adopted for girls aged 12 through 16.

1916
Scholarships to children of missionaries were first granted from the Margaret Fund, established from proceeds of the sale of the Margaret Home.

1918
Offering for foreign missions named for Lottie Moon.

The Calendar of Prayer was incorporated into *Royal Service.*

1919
WMU pledged to help raise $15 million for SBC $75 Million Campaign.

Sales of periodicals made WMU self-supporting.

1921
WMU headquarters moved to Birmingham, Alabama.

1922
World Comrades, a quarterly publication for GA, RA, and Sunbeams, began publication.

1925
WMU exceeded its $75 Million Campaign goal.

WMU urged SBC adoption of Cooperative Program.

1927
WMU became a major promoter of the Cooperative Program.

1929
Membership passed half million mark.

Young Woman's Auxiliary got their own magazine, *The Window of YWA.*

WMU president Ethlene Boone Cox became the first woman to address the Southern Baptist Convention.

1931
WMU gave nearly 50 percent of Cooperative Program contributions for the year.

1933
WMU adopted plan to retire Foreign Mission Board debts.

1934
Home missions offering named for Annie Armstrong.

1935
WMU Focus Weeks began.

1940
WMU pledged $1 million to retire SBC debts.

1941
First annual WMU Year Book in Spanish published.

1943
WMU exceeded SBC debt pledge.

1945
First $1 million Lottie Moon Christmas Offering.

1946
Ambassador Life was published for RA.

1949
WMU helped form SBC Inter-Agency Council.

1950
Membership passed 1 million mark.

Christmas in August began.

1951
WMU purchased a headquarters building in Birmingham, Alabama.

1953
First $1 million Annie Armstrong Offering taken.

Tell and *Sunbeam Activities* replaced *World Comrades.*

1956
WMU agreed to promote Lottie Moon Christmas Offering and Annie Armstrong Offering churchwide.

1957
Royal Ambassadors work transferred to Brotherhood.

1962
WMU let Foreign Mission Board and Home Mission Board decide how to spend offerings.

1964
Lottie Moon Christmas Offering collected $100 million in 76 years.

1966
WMU voluntarily adopted an agency program statement.

1968
Groups replaced circles.

1970
WMU adopted the SBC age-grading plan and launched new organizations:
Baptist Women for women aged 30 and above
Baptist Young Women for women aged 18–29
Acteens for girls in grades 7 through 12
Girls in Action for girls in grades 1 through 6
Mission Friends for preschool boys and girls

1972
WMU language missions was moved to WMU head-quarters from the Home Mission Board, which continued to fund it.

1976
Annie Armstrong Easter Offering collected $100 million in 64 years.

1977
WMU adopted SBC's Bold Mission Thrust plan.

WMU began regular churchwide missions activities.

WMU encouraged women to begin Big A Clubs for children in transitional communities.

First Acteens National Advisory Panel chosen.

Campus BYW launched.

Round Table Book Club began.

1978
Acteens Activators began.

A publication for preschoolers, *Mission Friends Share*, was introduced.

WMU and the HMB employed a WMU consultant to work in relationship with African America Baptists.

1981
WMU, with assistance from the Home Mission Board, published materials in Chinese, Korean, Japanese, Romanian, and Basic English.

First issue of *Our Missions World*, a monthly magazine in Basic English, was published.

1983
WMU produced videotapes for purchase or rental.

Baptist Nursing Fellowship was organized.

1984
WMU moved to new headquarters on top of New Hope Mountain, south of Birmingham, Alabama.

1985
New Hope Publishers imprint for generic missions material was established.

1988
WMU celebrated Centennial.

Lottie Moon Christmas Offering exceeded $1 billion in 100 years.

Age range for Baptist Young Women changed to include women aged 18 through 34.

1992
Annie Armstrong Easter Offering exceeded $500 million in 90 years.

1993
WMU adopted plan for second century in missions.

Since 1888 WMU helped raise more than $2 billion for SBC causes.

Baptist Nursing Fellowship began an overseas network.

Volunteer Connection was begun.

Project HELP was developed to target a specific social issue such as hunger, poverty, or abuse for concentrated study and action.

1995
WMU officially introduced coed organizations—Children in Action, Youth on Mission, and Adults on Mission.

The WMU Foundation was established to assure financial security for missions projects and WMU.

Mission Mosaic replaced *Royal Service* as magazine for women.

GA World introduced for older girls. *Discovery* remained the magazine for younger girls.

1996
WorldCrafts introduced its home party concept.

1997
Pure Water, Pure Love transferred from Brotherhood Commission to WMU.

1998
WMU launched a Web site, including interactive pages for all age levels.

2000
Sisters Who Care began as a program to develop Women on Mission organizations in Southern Baptist African American churches.

2003
The Mag replaced *Accent* as the magazine for teenage girls.

2004
Missions Leader^{sm} replaced *Dimension* as the magazine for WMU leaders.

2005
Christian Men's Job Corps ministries were beginning to open across the nation.

The Vision 2010 Task Force was enlisted to lay out broad directions for WMU's future.

Index

Thank you!

Your purchase of this book and other WMU products supports the mission and ministries of WMU. To find more great resources, visit our online store at www.wmustore.com or talk with one of our friendly customer service representatives at 1-800-968-7301.

WMU®
Discover the Joy of Missions℠
www.wmu.com